Sunday Painters

Flea Market, Garage Sale and Thrift Shop treasures.

By David Devensky

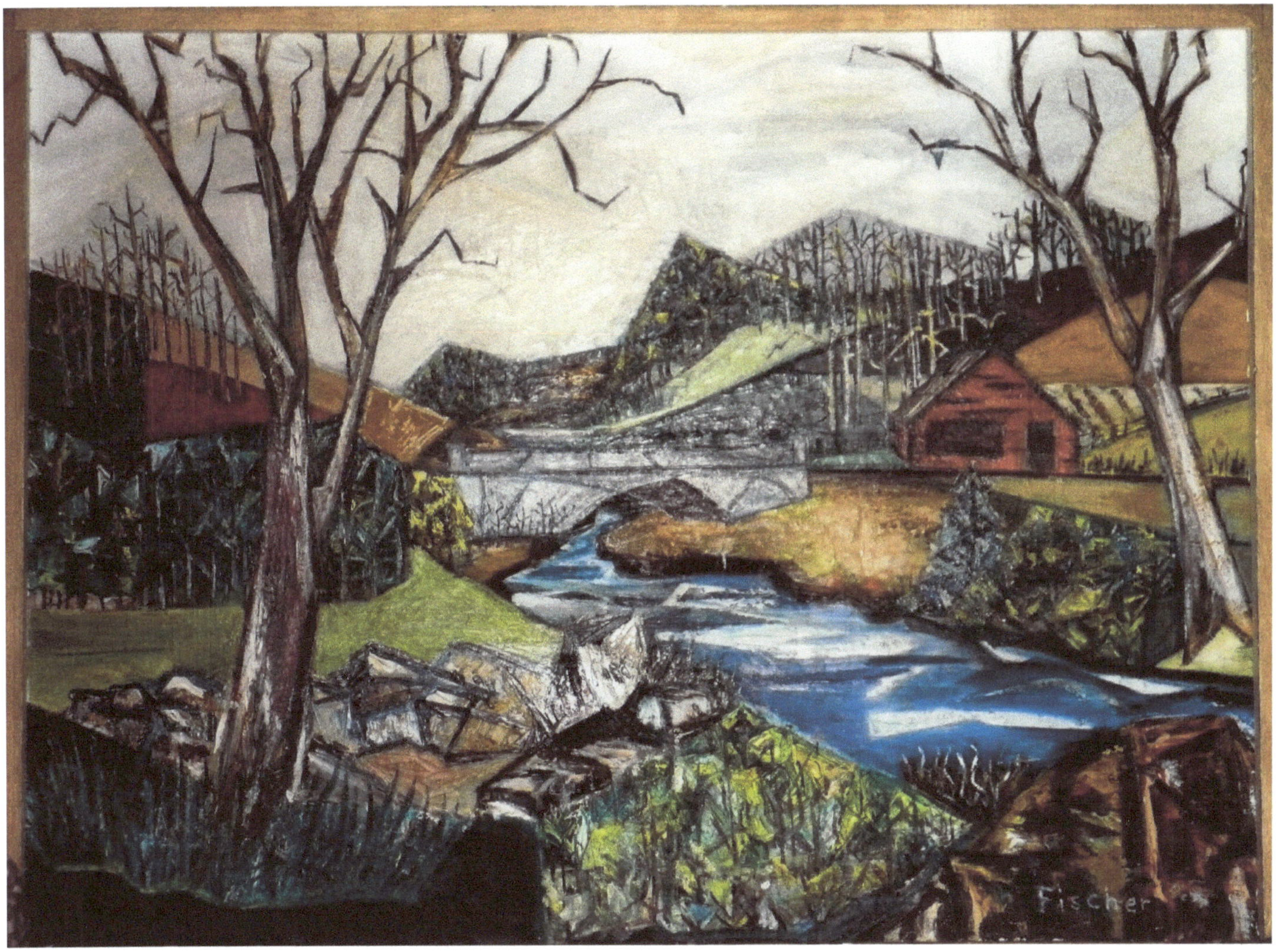

Here in intense color, a large geometric painting of a rural scene - cost $4.00

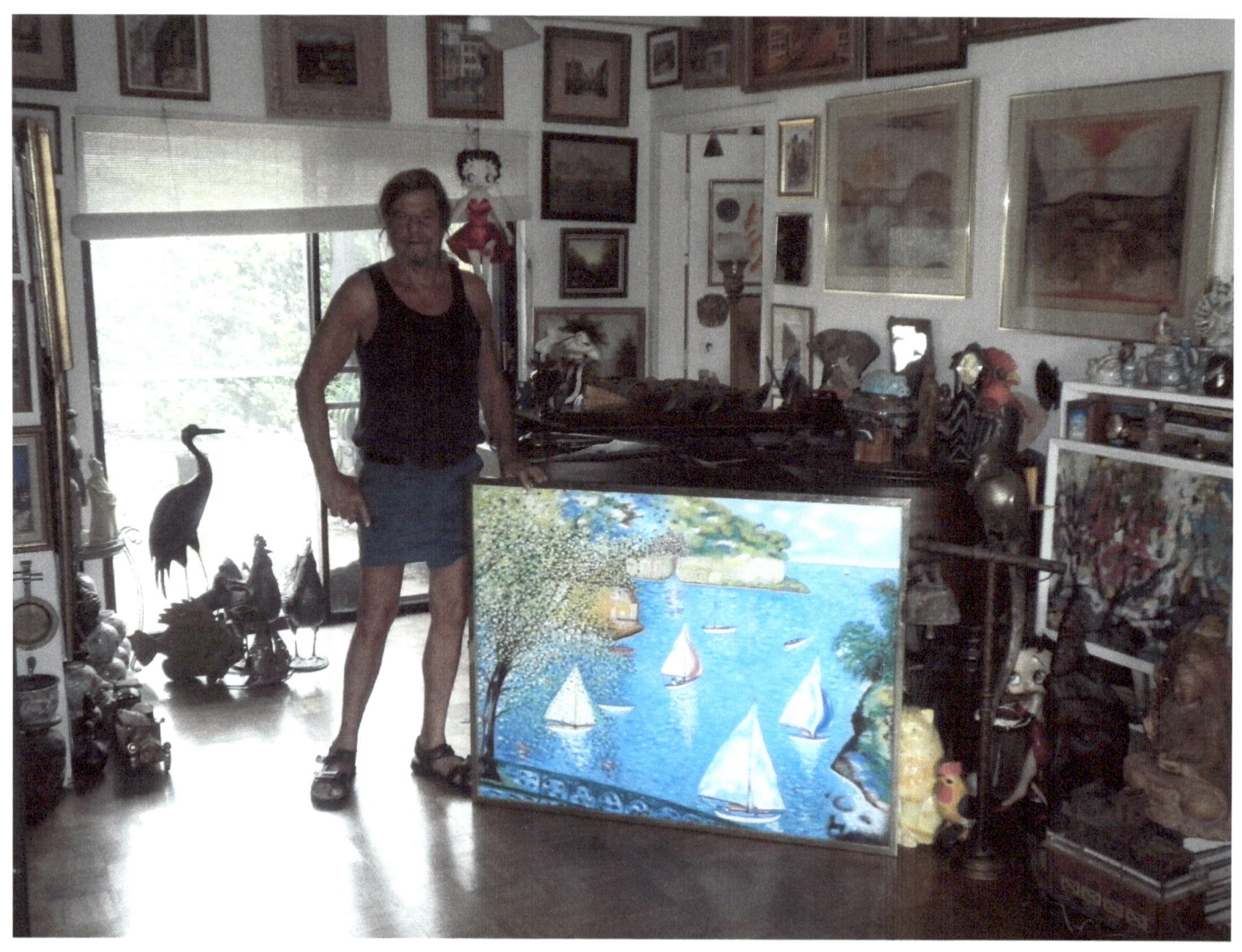

The author with a huge, charming oil, full of color and 'off' perspective, which he just purchased, at the local fleas, for ten bucks.

PREFACE

Now here's the scenario, as I see it. Middle Class couple retires to Florida. The man is usually, but not always, the collector. The retirement community offers little space so the couple rents a storage unit to store their unused treasures - treasures, too good for a variety of reasons, to let go. When man collector dies, his wife does one of two things; She attempts to sell Hal's old record collection or those 'horrible beer mugs', in happy hope of obtaining from their receipts, a new set of drapes for the living room. However, after a disappointing yard sale, after failing to interest auction houses and antiques store in these dismal treasures, REALITY strikes and our lady donates that whole heap of unwanted (i.e. misunderstood)"trash" to the local thrift store. Our second scenario might be more typical; she, out of guilt or nostalgia, continues to pay the storage unit fees, attempting, on occasion, to interest family and friends in its contents. When she, too, enters the deep ground, her yippy kids, who have no interest in anything less than a flat, Hi-Dif TV screen or a snazzy car, renege on the storage payments. Flea market venders who watch these storage units for default actions, now have their chance to gain control of their contents via an auction, which the storage company initiates to reclaim their rental fees. What comes out of these rental units can be truly unbelievable! One active dealer would bring different stuff each week. One week he would have sets of Lionel trains or a collection of ancient oil lamps while another would find him with an entire library of collectable art books or woodworking tools from the 1920s. Once, I purchased a collection of nine leather and vellum bound travel and cooking books from the 1700s at $5 apiece and on another, an absolutely authentic Inca burial shroud, at the cost of ten bucks!

I have been doing flea markets in South Florida for over 35 years, currently going four times a week. This, of course, is dispersed between hits on my favorite thrift shops and appearances at local yards sales - oh the glory of retirement! What I have amassed over the past decades has encompassed everything from ancient artifacts to delicate Chinese porcelain, vintage acoustic 78 records, to promotional stick fans embossed with color photos from WW1. Huge Art Deco vases to bronze sculptures and refined, collectable glassware, but the most fascinating indeed, for me, are the original paintings and quality prints that are constantly offered, many under $5 hence, the main theme and body of this book!

THRIFT SHOP TALES

Do it enough and one can get very good at "I. D.ing" your treasures' former owner! Several years back, I walked into a thrift shop just as they were putting out boxes and boxes of Classical LP recordings. Gleefully going through them, I was able to ascertain the taste of its former owner, the area he lived and during what time period he was formulating his collection. On another occasion, I even came across several records with the label of the small town's record shop I frequented. The labels were dated to the same time period when I was collecting and the owner, as was also my custom, had signed his name on the jackets. I did not recognize his name but, since we were in the same small town, shopping at the same record shop, I might very well have even seen him. Then the thought hit me – he probably died and his wife gave his collection away to that Thrift. An eerie feeling of my own mortality came over me.

One of the Thrifts I occasionally hit had a high shelf running around the entire perimeter of the store. On this occasion, that entire shelf displayed oil paintings by a single Sunday Painter – which I identified as the mother of the family. All were scenes painted in the 'Grand Piano Living Room' and portrayed her children at various times during their development. I could recognize the boys and girls growing and changing. There must have been a good 40 framed canvases of various sizes – a real family time capsule! The paintings themselves were colorful, competently conservative but uncreative. Its only value was to the family. I asked myself then, why or how did they get there?

Several weeks later, I revisited that Thrift and found the same paintings unsold. They were now stuffed together in a corner of that shelf. A month later, they were off the shelf and all jammed together into a remote corner of the shop. By my next visit, they were gone. I was, by then too sophisticated to believe that they'd finally found a buyer, but rather went the way of all "unsalables" – the large dumpster out in the back. A probable scenario; Mom and Dad sold the family house where they were prominently displayed, and moved to Florida. Their condo, too small to accommodate, the art work went into storage. After the couple 'kicked the bucket', their disinterested kids, unwilling to pay the storage fees, donated that "trash" to the local Thrift!

THE GOODWILL CLEARANCE STORE

In an obscure industrial section of West Palm Beach, there is a Goodwill Clearance Store. Few people know of its existence, or are able to find its 'off the beaten path' location (I found out about it from a friendly supervisor and had to call their unlisted phone number for traveling directions). A Clearance Store is a 'Last Chance Depository', a place to which all the area's Goodwill stores send their unsold goods. It also serves as a depot for all unwanted items that these Goodwill shops, due to their low sales and the store's high rental space, refuse to even stock. Clearance Stores like this are unusually frequented by 'Third World People'. Ours is a large, dimly lit, loft- type structure located in the Goodwill Depot building in the West Palm Beach industrial section. Here you will find no frills. There are no racks from which clothing hang. There are no shelves where books and records are placed. Paintings and prints are piled high against the wall, or stuffed into large wheeled bins. One will experience a riot when Juan wheels in an open bin of shoes. On my first visit, I held my head in horror when I saw a rushing, belligerent crowd of beefy, large women throw themselves upon a cart of shoes. Grabbing and screaming, they threw the shoes down in the territory by their feet, only later to examine and fling their selections into their shopping carts (here, I should mention that clothing and shoes are sold by the pound and not by the item, its condition, or quality). Often, fights break out, hence management, in order to quell the insanity, decided to place a tarp over carts containing the more desirable items in the hope that their 'gentle clientele' would not know if that bin contained the highly desirable shoes or was just a bin of men's underwear. The tarp failed to stop the insanity. Often, the police have been called and once, the shop was shut down. For a while, the 'book and picture people' usually acted better than the more utilitarian 'shoe and clothing crowd' but, during the last couple of years of my long visiting tenure, they too, like the record nuts, became insane.

All clients 'stage-up' by the door until opening at 8.00am. Personally, I try to arrive after this chaotic opening scene. I once witnessed a 'pig-faced beast' kick another 'horror monster' who 'pig -faced' felt was intruding on her place in line. Juan, who opens the door, tries to keep the crowd controlled as he says "good morning" to the "animals" who, ignoring him, charge forward. Then there is an insane rush to grab a shopping cart and dash toward the bin or area of one's choice. Then comes the elbowing out of your neighbor and the aggressive 'grab grab, load your carts'. Being an intellectual, I have special fascination with the 'book people'. When most of their stock is exhausted, these 'bookmen' (actually there are as many 'book women' involved as bookmen) take out their computer/scanner and check each book for its resale value. This is a rapid-fire process, as these 'book people' dump rejected book after rejected book back into the bin from which they were initially taken. Their speed comes from the fact that, in a few more minutes, Juan will be bringing out another cart which might very well be stuffed with books. During this 'wacko process' some wear face masks to protect themselves from the mountains of erupting dust that form. What they returned to these bins are treasures of the first order, books that do not meet the popular demand, books that their computers have told them are selling low, slow or not at all; books so rare that their prosaic computer programs have no record of them. Although many of these 'bookmen' are smart, they have little feeling for the commodity in which they deal. Since they realize that I represent no commercial or competitive threat to them, we have enjoyed a 'fun' relationship. On more than one occasion, I would mock their mad insane grabbing with "Gentle, Gentlemen, Oh my God Gentlemen, please observe the basic decorum of decency." I laugh internally as I see how little my humor has affected them! If their chosen book does not pass the criterion of commercial value, rare and fascinating book treasures are returned. What I have gleaned from the rejects of these "crazies" is exceptional.

TREASURES FROM THE DEPTH OF INSANITY

On my very first trip to the Clearance Store I had a glorious hit! I am a passionate record collector and have found it harder and harder to find 78s from the acoustic era (records manufactured during the late 1890s to 1925). There, in the store's record bin, were hundreds of them; 78rpm recordings scattered helter skelter in the albums that they were originally placed in a hundred years ago. Some were piled up in their original albums while others loose in stacks. Many were cracked and broken due to the way they were dumped into the bin or by other record collectors after a rare Beatle pressing. I was able to save and buy 200 of them at 15 for a dollar. The next bin over had VHS tapes which fetched under 10 cents each (15 for a buck), CDs and DVDs were 50 cents and a dollar. Oh what great fun I had!

PROCURING PAINTINGS AND PRINTS

As I mentioned before, clothing and shoes are sold by the pound, books are priced via their hard or soft cover status while records, DVDs and tapes, by quantity. The story is different for paintings and prints. Here, it is their size that determines their price. Small pictures fetch $1 or less, medium $2, and large to huge $3 or $4 each. Again, the quality of the pictures has little to do with the price. One can buy a large awful painting for $3 as well as an exquisite small one for a buck.

Throughout the years, I have discovered a few oddities about the various Goodwill stores and how their policies affect the stock of the clearance store. From my experience, each Goodwill store has its own individual pricing policy. Certain Goodwill stores tend to price similar items higher than others. Whether this is due to venue (i.e. a more affluent area will pay more) or the individual quirks of management, I do not know. For instance, the Goodwill closest to me always tends to price higher than others. Also, prices for all the Goodwill stores, aside from special sales or Senior Day, are never reduced. If an item remains unsold for a designated period of time, it is unceremoniously shipped right off to the Clearance Store. This appears the standard policy for all their stores.

A case in point; my Goodwill had a wonderful extra-large oil of a Florida type swamp scene (see #13). They put it out for $99 and no matter where they hung it, or how they attempted to feature it, it did not sell. Instead of the more logical idea of reducing its price in hope of a sale, they, after a month, shipped it off to the Clearance Store. There I discovered it and bought it for three bucks! This defect in their perception has gleefully allowed me treasure after treasure at prices that are basically gifts! Once, I even used the threat of the Clearance Store to get a supervisor to reduce the price of an unsold watercolor (see # 26) by remarking that my offer would look better in their cash register than in the cash register of the Clearance Store!

As you will discover in the upcoming pages, the Clearance Store is the cure and the remedy for the incompetent insanity of Goodwill pricing and policy.

FLEA MARKET ECCENTRICS

Our local flea market is held four times a week in a Drive-In Movie parking lot. If you're not there before 7a.m., you probably missed out on most of the choice items. However, since the market is fairly large, and no one seeker can be everywhere at the same time, a late arrival may stumble upon a "hit" by appearing 'on the scene' just as a seller is removing a treasure from his car or truck. There is also the phenomenon of 'various prices at different times' for the same piece. Here a seller initially asks a high price for an item ('high balling') but, after several pass it by, he sobers into reality allowing a later arriver to pick up this gem for a reasonable or "gift" amount. On one instance, a seller asked $50 for an interesting painting that I might have been pleased to purchase for $15. Less than an hour later, I saw another seeker with the same painting. He told me he too was asked $50 but laughed and was able to buy it for $5. If he was the early bird and I the late, it would be me who own it at a "gift price" (shockingly, I was able to buy this exact picture for $10 – see # 12)

However, all said, it is still the "early bird" who generally "gets the worm" even if he has to make a return trip to see if 'seller-boy' has regained his pricing senses. Recently, I just missed picking up an original Florida Highwaymen painting by seconds. One of our regular seekers was just a few steps ahead of me. With her sharp eye, she picked up this treasure for $25, turning it over to another within the hour, for $350! I was very happy for her for she, like so many other early morning seekers, make or supplement their income, from these flea market-thrift shop -garage sale hunts.

Unlike most of these early morning fanatics, I am not interested in 'turning over' or selling my finds. I basically buy what delights me with little eye for a profit or an Ebay sale. Although I am knowledgeable of values, it is not my motivating factor. I can see much beauty in a chipped piece of porcelain, a broken woodcarving, a worn book or a damaged picture while others, because its condition has caused a commercial loss in value, will pass it by. Sometimes an item is so unique one can only get it in the condition it appears, or not at all. It is these original treasures that appeal to me. "Welcome aboard," I say, "Especially if you'll only cost me a couple of bucks"! I guess here it is like that old adage about "looking at the donut and not at its hole"

THE DIFFERENT TYPES OF SELLERS

We look for the seller who just cleaned out Grandma's attic and is eager to 'dump' this old brass school bell for the price of a six-pack or a chicken dinner. Many of them are unaware of value or care little about it. Once, I got from this type of seller, several exquisite oriental carvings -in both wood and stone- for as little as 50 cents apiece! These sellers usually appear once and are seldom seen again. Then there are the sellers who make an occasional appearance when they fall into a supply of stuff from which they feel they might make a flea market buck. Sometimes their own ignorance is a factor which can ruin their sale. This seller isn't the type that would watch Antiques Roadshow, and feels that if he never saw an item, it must be rare and have great value. Once, one of these' fly-by-nights' had a pile of old one-sided 78s recordings. He felt they were rare treasure and should command a high price when in reality, they are quite common and of little interest to the overwhelming majority. Their value, in top condition, would be a buck each – which should be liberally discounted for quantity purchase. Since, I knew I was perhaps the only buyer interested in old records like these , I knew that he should have been happy to sell them to me but he stood his 'highball' ground and I 'walked'. If he had been one of the standard weekly sellers, I would have bided my time and, after he got tired of bringing these discs week after week -without a sale, I would have make him an offer of 50 cents a shot but he was a one-shot 'fly-by-nighter' and a sale was impossible. This incident was especially haunting for on the following day, I discovered these same records, flung into the dumpster - thrown there probably because he didn't want to 'lug that trash home'. All were broken beyond repair, a sacrilegious tragedy.

As mentioned before, there are the sellers who buy out storage units due to their owner's unpaid rental bills. Here, anything can turn up and if a rapport has been established between you and the vender, interesting stuff at fair prices will be coming your way! Here we have a sensitivity game between seller and buyer. A friendly good humor and wit are imperative. There are sellers that I enjoy and who, hopefully enjoy me while others (usually the ones who "highball" you on everything) I avoid, sometimes not even gazing at their offerings. If I was quoted a 'too high' price for a picture and I noticed it unsold, week after week, I might, with cheerful non aggressive humor say "Hey, I didn't know you wanted to start an art gallery. I thought that these pictures are for sale!" I've also learned never to degrade an item but praise it saying; "It's very nice but a bit too much for what I want to spend, or "It's truly lovely... too bad it has that long tear down the side".

A little knowledge is a dangerous thing, especially in the flea market and that is true from both the aspect of the sellers – who price trash too high or the buyers – who though ignorance, either overpay or buy a reproduction as an original. When a seller, though his own ignorance, feels he has the Czarina's Crown Jewels (while in essence they are made of paste) little can be done until he himself sees his own folly. Besides, a flea market is just that: a flea market. It is not an uptown gallery or an elegant shop hence, pricing here must be a bargain. Once I had purchased an excellent large watercolor from a dealer who initially demanded $45 (see # 25).This might have been a 'steal' from an 'on-the-avenue' art shop but a bit out of line for a flea market. I eventually got it for a more realistic $15, when, week after week, it remained unsold. I once bought a huge bizarre oil painting which many others looked at but didn't buy (see #14). Its seller, seeing how, week after week, it was physically deteriorating, sold it to me, over the screaming objections of his wife, for ten dollars. I am sure his motivation was to salvage something from it before it became completely destroyed. Here, a good eye can easily analyze repairable items from those that are unsalvageable or too costly to restore.

One funny incident got me a huge 'swamp scene' oil painting for 6 bucks (see #19). The lady was asking $10 for it, a true gift. Suddenly, another customer held up a pair of shoes and asked "How Much"? My lady replied $5 upon which I said "I'll give you $5" (referring to the painting).To my astonishment, she took my offer seriously but said she had to call her friend and OK it with her. We settled on 6 bucks. I had trouble fitting this treasure into my car as I trembled with joy.

A FEW CRAZIES AND CLOWNS

I must say, I do get great pleasure from my fellow flea market nuts! Some of the eccentrics I've encountered throughout the years are as original as they are bizarre! A few I have given nicknames like: Roger-Dodger, an elderly man who would dart around the fleas, buying and buying and eventually unable to manage the load of stuff he acquired. Many times I would see him struggle and carry his burden to his car – a huge station wagon which literally reeked of decaying trash. Eventually, 'Roger-Dodger' had to use a walker but still this 91 year old was able to hop and run with the best of them! About a year ago he disappeared from the Flea Market scene and I found out he had to enter an assisted living facility. When we gave him a call, he had only one complaint; "This place is just full of old people!"

Many of these eccentrics are knowledgeable with unique personalities. Here I will mention a few of the more entertaining ones. Alfredo is one of the Flea Markets Stars. He gave up his lawn maintenance business to follow the path of playing in his rock band - which he also books into local venues. He has an exceptional sense of humor and darts about the Flea Market on an electrical cart in an attempt to be everywhere at the same time. He would ask a seller for the price of an item. After hearing it, he might respond with something like "Does that also include breakfast"? I found it difficult to top his wit. Once, during a rare Florida cold snap, I saw him wearing a ratty overcoat. I couldn't resist going up to him with "I known that overcoat; it once belonged to a family that died from scarlet fever." He answered me by saying that he just found a half eaten candy bar in one of its pockets which he had just 'wolfed' down! He especially likes paintings but often fails to sell them. On the wooden fence surrounding his back yard he has hung up these pictures, calling it his "Wall of Shame." There they would be displayed– in the heat and rain, giving him and his guests' months of viewing pleasure before melting away, only to be replaced by other mistakes!

Don is a different sort. Tall, good looking with silver white hair, one could mistake him for a bank president or a business executive but he is a super art expert who freely shares his knowledge with all. This sometime works to his disadvantage, for by educating his fellow seekers in what to look for, or enlightening the seller in the true value of an item, he increases his competition and has to pay more than he might have from the sellers whom he had just educated. Nevertheless, he constantly finds items which he has auctioned off for thousands of dollars. Recently he found an item which, at a major auction, brought $80,000. I have seen him almost every time I go the 'Fleas' and often met him at thrift shops and art museums. He is a true art lover, perhaps too free and generous with his knowledge and experience, for his own good.

FINAL THOUGHTS ON THE SEARCH

As I have already mentioned, I, unlike most of the buyers, seldom acquire any item to 'turnover', hence it doesn't bother me to get up at 5:30 am, drive to the 'Market', spent a good hour walking it several times and find little or nothing. What would bother me is not to go at all and wonder if I missed out on anything! By going, and going at the correct time, I can see that life has not passed me by! The regular sellers, too, are just as fanatic in not leaving any stone unturned. Many do not open their selling sites until they too, walk about, hoping to 'snag' a treasure from what another more naive sellers might have brought. These finds are usually 'turned over' that morning, after being investigated via their hand- held computers, which are viewed at 'dawn's early light' via a hand -held flashlight!

IS IT WORTH BEING A SELLER?

From a purely financial aspect, I must say "No." True, many sellers have honestly told me that "last Sunday they made $300." However, if one would take into account the amount of time it would take to load up their van, the driving time and gas spent to get to the selling location, the hour plus wait at the flea market to be conducted to their site - and the charge for the same (it's $20 here for a Sunday), then unload and setup their items, spend six to eight hours in the hot humid Florida sun only to reload again, drive back home and unload. Couple this with the original cost of the items they sold, along with the time and effort it took them to originally acquire them and then the many days they made - with the same above effort- little or nothing (either due to bad weather, or poor attendance) then that $300, indeed, seems a small sum. The end result, I fear, would be less than minimum wage.

Personally, I can't see buying a picture for $10 and selling it at the market for the same price I paid or perhaps, not at all. A flea market, as mentioned above, does not command the prices an antique shop or an art gallery would fetch. A matter of fact, many antique and gallery owners regularly 'glean' these markets and thrifts for bargain price stock. If I ever were to sell my collections, I would do so at better class antique or art shows. True, I would have to pay more to get a spot but along with that comes a more affluent clientele. While spending the identical time as I would for a flea market setup, my profit and sale chances are greatly improved. Most of these upper class customers are either unaware of the 'experience' of a flea market or thrift shop or are disinterested in wasting their time, at an ungodly hour, in hope to improve their exacting collections. This clientele, I feel, would prefer to look for quality items of their individual interest, conveniently collected and well displayed as these antique and art shows offer. Flea markets give no guarantee that you will find any addition to your nautical collection. One must be open to what appears there – one week finding an art book, the next a vintage Lionel train set. Those in single-minded pursuit best stay with the more expensive but specialized dealers that these better class shows and shops offer.

SP-#1 - Here is the Huge Goodwill $99 Oil painting they couldn't sell and, rather than reducing the price, they shipped it off to the Clearance Store where I picked it up for $3.00! A huge; 4 & ¼ X 2 & ½ feet.

SP-#2 - Here's the 1955 watercolor I cajoled a Goodwill Supervisor to reduce by threatening her with the Clearance Store!

SP-#3 - First offered to me and others for $50, a late flea market Seeker purchased it from the frustrated Seller for $5. A few weeks later, I was able to snag it for $10! A strange Middle Eastern picture with Chinese boats.

SP-#4 - This wonderful American Southwest Native American watercolor was brought, week after week by a Seller who wanted $45. I was able to make him see the light and he took $15!

SP-#5 - I can still hear the squawking of the Seller's wife when he sold me this huge 4 & ¼ X 3 & ½ feet for ten bucks!

SP-#6 - The huge 5 X 3 & ¼ foot 'swamp scene' for which a flea market cell phone call got it for me for six bucks!

SP-#7-11 - Here we have five colorful, but rather prosaic pictures - An arched stone bridge over a country river, two rather stiff children playing with a ball in a pleasant meadow, a little boy leading a little girl to a sweet county stream, a house by the road and a picture of dull, blurry cypress tree along a dismal country road. Interest and value could be increased by adding a lynched hanged man dangling from the bridge painting, a lit fuse on the children's ball turning it into a bomb ready to exploded (here, one could add on the grass, the unseen arm of the child in yellow), a large knife in the little boy and girl picture (or perhaps we can add a sinister alligator in the stream), a trail of blood from the topsy-turvy swing to the house while a limp, half eaten arm hangs from the window sill, all to the obvious interest of the hovering birds, and either a funeral procession traveling the desolate cypress tree road or better, a nuclear bomb explosion off in the dismal distance of road's end! Sinister and bizarre touches to be sure, but now we have created, with very little effort, pictures that have more depth, wonder and interest than they originally conveyed! Total cost; Bridge Picture - $4.00, Children in Meadow -$2.39 (with tax and Senior Day discount), Little Boy leads Little Girl – six bucks, The House by the road and the Cypress trees pictures ran five apiece. All were purchased in different Thrifts shops/Fleas and at different times.

SP-#12 - At my local Goodwill, I came across these two gems. Although different sizes, they may be put together to make a fascinating Expressionist scene that Van Gogh might have conceived had he lived longer. One can only wonder what was in that artist's mind when he created these haunting images. I took a chance and waited a few days for Senior Day where they fetch about $7 each.

 SP-13 & 14 - Running out of wall, door and furniture space to hang pictures, I came up with an ingenious idea for these pseudo Florida Highwaymen style paintings - the area right above my shower! True, I no longer shower but what does it matter when one can display such interesting beauty!

SP-#15-17 - We have here three intense pictures! The take-off on Cézanne is a huge 3 & ½ by 2 & ½ feet. The other two are slightly smaller. All came framed except the smallest one. With such an intense picture, a simple black frame might have been best but since it was an odd size, I was lucky to find the size in this intense frame at the Fleas for $3. Hence, I have created a more intensive experience by placing an intense picture within a more intense frame – a real visual WOW!

SP-#18 - Who could resist this wonderfully fame colorful toucan for $15 – 3 & ½ X 2 & ½ feet!

SP-#19 - Here's a case of internet folly. This huge flea market purchase (4 & ¼ X 3 & ¼ feet) is signed "Day". There is a listed artist named Day but the style doesn't match. Was it an earlier work? Thinking not, I'll still enjoy my $15 swimming swans!

SP-#20- Another huge oil of Swimming Swans but when I picked it up - at a 'Thrift' for ten bucks,-it appeared too heavy. At home I investigate why. The oil is directly painted on top the frame's glass! A true first!

SP-#21 – I know I overpaid a bit for this surreal gem but I wanted to study it. It is an actual painting but not as antique as it appears. I feel the frame and the board the picture was painted on is cast. The color scheme of both picture and frame are unified. The picture itself is wonderfully 'hokey'. Notice the lack of perspective between the cottage and woman on shore and the huge row boat in the water!

SP-#22 - A wonderful sensitively colored Florida scene put up in the Clearance Store bin for $2

SP-#23 - Another sensitive Clearance Store treasure, also at bin's bottom and $2 without tax!!

SP-#24 - This Florida night scene was $15 at an antique shop. I was haunted by it and could find nothing on him until I did a search on Ebay. Here, a seller offered another picture by him. There was a picture on the painting's back which showed a label containing much biographical information!

SP-#25 - A large, Florida Everglades scene containing a hand written note on its back stating that the artist painted it at age 91. Oh, this treasure! Cost 6 bucks!

SP-#26 -Who could refused this wonderfully framed tropic scene of birds in a swamp. True, it's probably not in Florida but for ten bucks who cares!

SP-#27- An intensely colored oil of a figure walking by a river. Price: 4 bucks plus tax!

SP-#28 - A Flea Market Seller offered me this fine framed watercolor for one dollar. I couldn't pay him quick enough!

SP-#29 - This huge 3X4 Sunday Painter's fantasy took my breath away from the first second I saw it! The deliberate 'out of perspective' of the cottage makes such an interesting contracts to the sculpted texture of the mountain range's bizarre colors. A first class museum piece, it was heavily damaged with canvas rips and a missing corner. The vendor wanted it out and sold it to me for one dollar!!

SP-#30 - This haunting moonlight mountain scene has sailboats off in the background. It was on sale for seven bucks and one can only wonder who was the artist of this, and my many other treasures?

SP-#31 - How bizarre is this American South West oil with its two huge dancing Kachina dolls!

SP-#32 & 33 - Naivety at its best! Two colorful pictures by two different Sunday Painters!

SP-#34 - These two exceptional oil paintings, with similar color schemes, were bought, for slightly over five dollars each but at different times at the Fleas. The larger one on the left was sold to me by a woman who said her sister was a curator at a museum...hummm!

SP-#35 - A wonderful ,watercolor portraying a rural Black scene. Note that the cardboard mat has been painted brown to simulate a wooden frame. Purchased for a Flea Market dollar, I decided to "protect the innocent" and reframe all!

SP#36- The top half of this powerful painting portrays a country water mill while its bottom has its reflection - a standard technique practiced by all painters. However, the intensity of its color and form reveal the strong personality of our Sunday Painter.

SP-#37- One can only guess the story behind the subject of this haunting painting, purchased for under $3.

SP-#38. Written in Spanish on the back of this desolate canvass; "Los Anos Pasen" ("The Years Pass"). My cost : $2.

SP-#39 - A large exquisite Florida oil dated 1975.

SP-#40 - One does not need much imagination to see a story in this huge painting (3 & ¾ ' x 2 & ¾ '). Amidst a bucolic scene of greenery and nature, a Civil War Union Soldier informs a woman of the death of her loved one. This colorful, but rather naïve and stiffly painted oil, captures a moment in time - the very second before the woman hears or comprehends the news. Again, this huge canvas and frame was a gift at 3 bucks at the Clearance Store.

SP-#41 - Sunday Painters have the freedom to choose noncommercial subjects. Here's an oil painting by "Beatrice' of an unusual fish! Cost was under nine dollars.

SP-#42 - Here we can see how important the frame is for "setting-off" a painting!

SP-#43 - Notice how skillfully our Sunday Painter integrates in this large canvas, the form of the rocky mountains with that of the trees. Picked it up, without a frame, for two bucks!

SP-#44 – This grimacing slice of apple pie has an attitude!

SP-#45 – A wonderful, desolate scene.

SP-#46 – This huge colorful swamp scene cost under $5 at the Goodwill Clearance Store.

SP-#47 – A wonderfully ,composed, color fantasy that can only exist in the creative mind of a Sunday Painter.

SP-#48 – A personal painting for me indeed. Like this Sunday Painter's tree, perhaps we both feel we stand apart from the mainstream.

SP-#49 – A bleakly, beautiful 'arctic-like' coastal scene. Something so haunting about this one buck treasure!

SP- #50 &51 – Two different concepts of America's Southwest scenery.

SP- #52 - Another huge treasure (3' X 4'), supposedly of the Spanish Treasured Coast.

SP-#53 – The buildings on this bizarre town's street seem to scream horror with their eye-like windows, paining doors and bleeding colors. Note the modern telephone wires above!

SP-#54 – The frantic intense colors and motions well forgives the picture's awkward technique.

SP- #55 and 56 - Now here's an oddity! If you don't like the fantasy painting on one side, just flip it over for a more traditional view of Venice taped to its back!

SP-#57 - The buildings in this exceptional Venice scene ($6 at my Flea) seem to cry out in their distortion as they sink into the sea!

SP-#58 – I suspect that this dramatically colorful scene was painted by the same artist as #64 & 66 since they were all bought at the same time and from the same flea market vender.

SP-#59 & 60 - Here are two 'melting color' pictures, one from the Fleas, the other, from a 'Thrift'.

SP-#61 & 62 Sunday Painters –with no commercial concerns – can let their imagination go wild! Here's a portrait featuring a rusting bucket and another of a distorted sea-side staircase.

SP-#63 - How strange is the subject of this picture! It shows the moment a wild bird dies and falls down into his jungle habitat.

SP-#64 & 66 - Here are two very different portraits, which I expect is by the same artist. A pretty girl, bathed in an impressionist mirror of light, is caught in the act of preparing herself for a date (?) – while a French slaughter house worker (?) glances us a wonderful smirk, his sinister meat hook ready and poised over his left shoulder. A Sunday Painter at her (?) colorful and insightful best! Both of these portraits have 'study images' on their reverse. My flea market cost? A gift at $2.50 each!!

SP-#65 – A super oddity!! Virtually the same scene, probably painted by the same artist, but found in three different Thrifts Shops and at different times!

SP-#66 – see SP- #64

SP-#67 - A sweet small scene of a new arrival on the planet Earth.

SP-#6 8 & 69 - Although Frida Kahlo painted self portraits with parrots and monkeys – she never did these two gems. They are the creative fantasy of one of our more talented Sunday Painters!

SP-70 – Another art work by the talented but bizarre "Beatrice"! Purchased for under four bucks!

SP-#71 – A wonderfully framed oil of a floating flower pot!

SP-#72 – Two colorful primitive studies in perspective by the same Sunday Painter.. But Wait! Why does the road in both pictures (more obvious in the picture on the left) appear to transcend through that huge mountain and why are the houses deliberately fighting the perspective established by the tree lines? Is our primitive Sunday Painter making a statement? At $2.50 apiece, it's worth an investigation!

SP-#73 – Again our creative Beatrice comes through with a road lined with dead tress while daisies bounce in front and greenery appears in the future.

SP-#74 – A dissolute, forsaken village seems held together by a thin lifeline of electrical wires.

SP-#75- Here in this native village, the only way out appears the raging river.

SP-#76- A true master has created a scene which changes color and emphasis as the light on it reflexes.

SP-#77 - – An unusual view of a great city from a barren island across the water.

SP-#78 – Here our nature scene, with its free -flying birds, contrast against the imprisoned fenced porch.

SP-#79 –This large, wonderful Florida night swamp scene was gifted to me for under 7 bucks.

SP-#80 – When I first saw this colorful oil of a little girl collecting flowers in a green meadow I felt that it was a Sunday Painter doing homage to his daughter. Studying it however, I sensed a greater depth

SP- #81 & #82 –The author turns two of his prosaic record shelves into art galleries.

SP- #83 – I could not capture the intense colors of this 'change of the leaves' oil. On the back, all is confirmed; "Blue Ridge (Mountains) autumn 1/10/85"

SP- #84 –When I bought this large powerful ocean scene (with a nude fisherman ready to cast his net into the mayhem) I wondered where was its location. A tear in the brown paper on the canvas back had my answer; "White Sands Point. Kona Bay Island, Aug. 1987".

SP- #85- One can feel and smell the cool air of this New England autumn.

SP-#86 – This large and powerful ocean scene cost me 6 bucks.

SP- #87 –The creative colors and shapes of this well framed sailboat trilogy totally belie its 4 dollar price.

SP - #88 – Our gal Beatrice is influenced here, I feel, by Albert P. Ryder's many late 19thCentury 'boats in the moonlight' paintings. Here, it is her own color and form that create a gem.

SP-#89 - One can only wonder what the purpose is of these igloo-type huts that line both sides of this broad river. A pleasing picture it is!

SP-#90 – A spider and a flower emerge forth from a misty waterfall – truly unique!

SP-#91 – On occasion, a Sunday Painter will copy a master. Here one effectively does so, but only painting the center section of Van Gogh's "Crows in a Cornfield." Since it is signed- hence complete- we can justifiably assume that it was never intended as the center of a triptych. His valiantly captured brush strokes and colors of that master, comprise the picture's main appeal.

SP -#92 - I bought a series of fine quality watercolors (as this example testifies) from a woman in the Flea Market who was selling them for her neighbor and at incredibly cheap prices (about a dollar each). It seems that all of these watercolors were painted by the neighbor's father. When I asked her why her neighbor was selling her father's work and at such reasonable prices, she hesitated, then blurted out "I don't think he was a very good father." That aside, he was – as all can see- a very good watercolorist!

SP-#93 – A smug and smirking tiger made me laugh enough to part with five bucks!

SP-#94– A well composed winter scene with a hopeful bright yellow bird perched above.

SP-#95 and #96 - I have seen this scene before; black youths in Florida's wilderness. Perhaps scenes like this were inspired by the recent respect afforded to the art of the Florida Highwaymen paintings. In our first oil we see a black youth going, or coming from – it's hard to tell, a fishing adventure. Even without the tell-tale palm trees, the flat look of the land and the native slash pines speak "Florida." In our second oil, our boy rides a skid in an Everglades setting. Both are charming and wonderful – two important additions to my Florida collection!

SP - #97 – A fat content cat has overtones of Japanese influence. I love him!

SP- #98 – A fantasy? An intensively crowded, walled medieval city is seen from its barren surroundings. I got it for a fiver!

SP- #99 – Here we do indeed have an eerie picture of s young girl sitting by a bleak sinister sea. Her white pink clad body contrasts menacingly against the black blue sky.

SP-#100 – Not to appear 'corny', I end my little book with a sail into the sunset! The boats look Chinese but the sunset belongs to the world. A haunting and beautifully captured moment!

SP #01

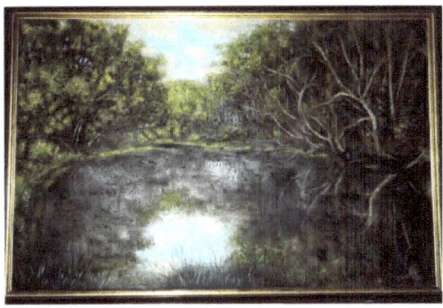

SP #02

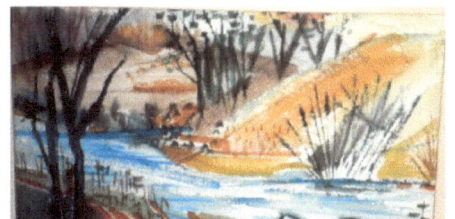

SP #03

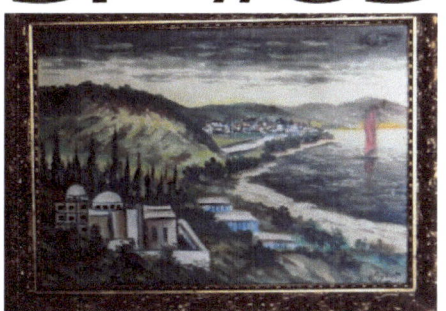

SP #04

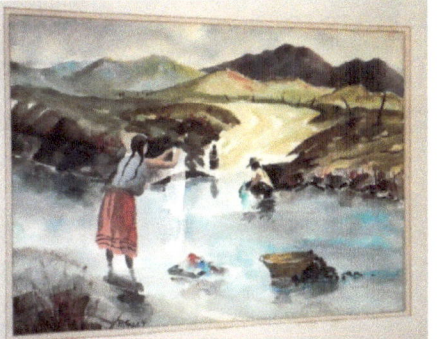

SP #05

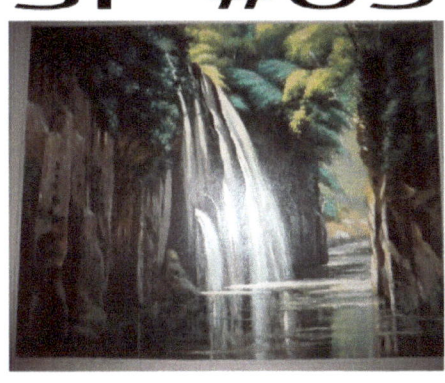

SP #06

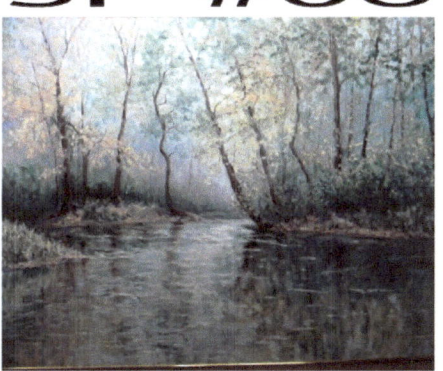

SP #07

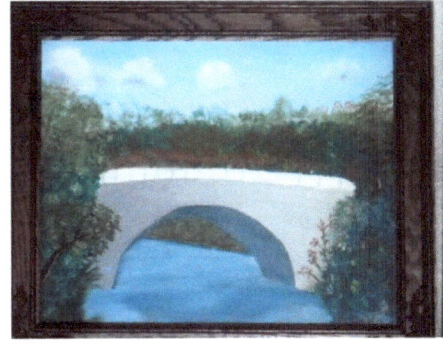

SP #08

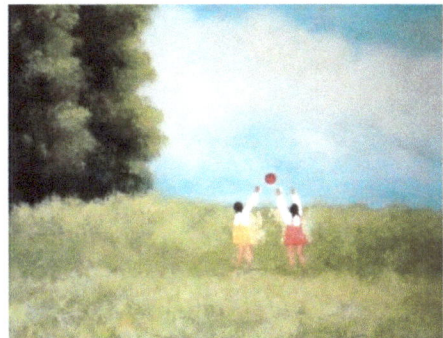

SP #09

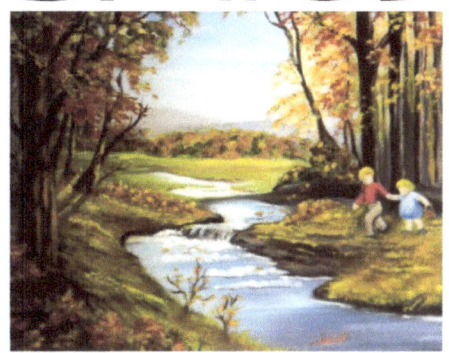

SP #10

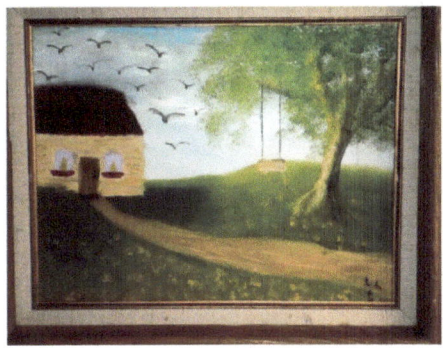

SP #11

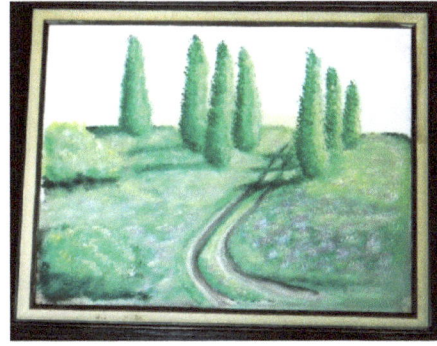

SP #12

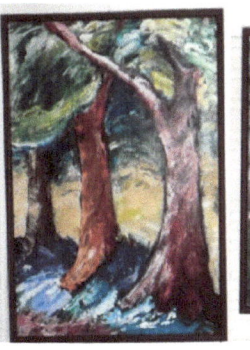 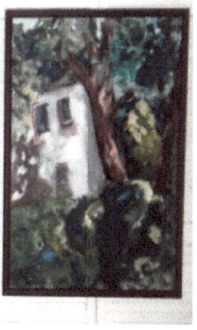

SP #13

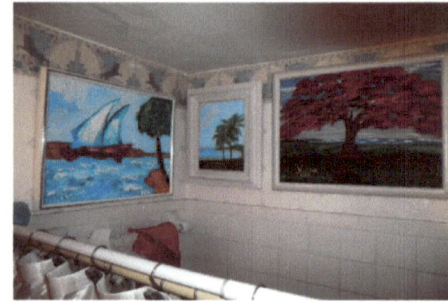

SP #14

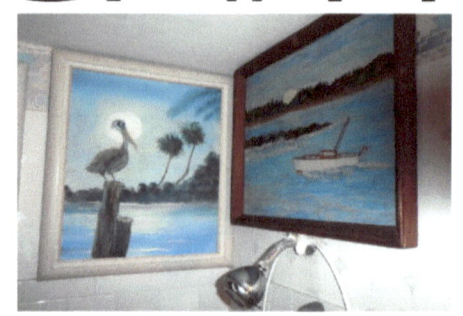

SP #15

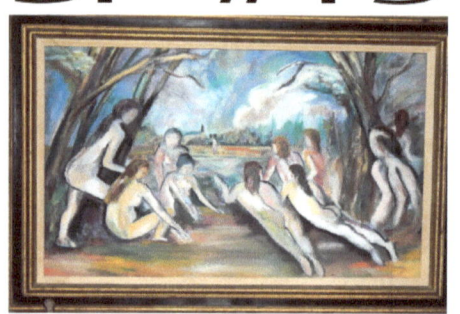

SP #16

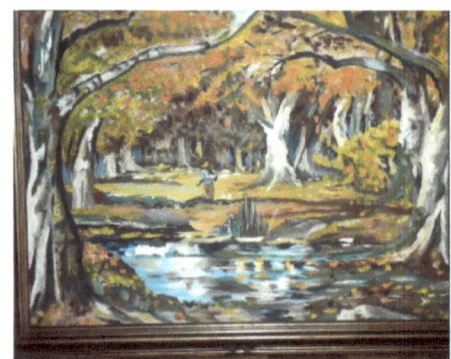

SP #17

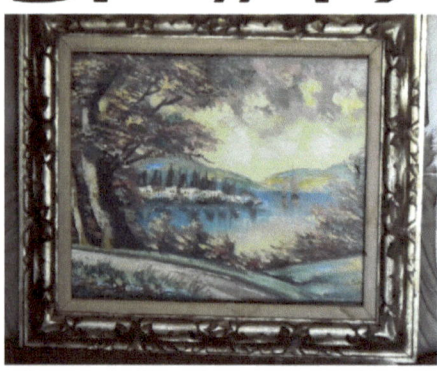

SP #18

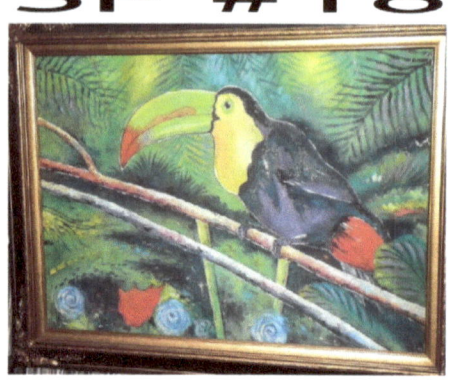

SP #19

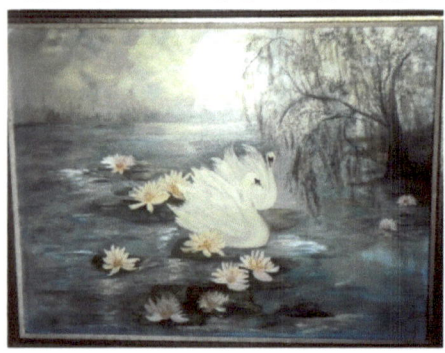

SP #20

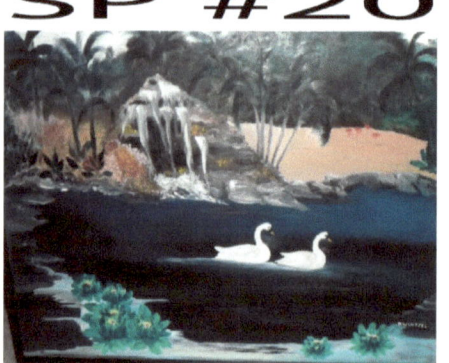

SP #21

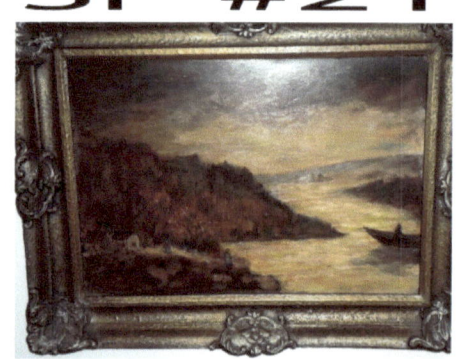

SP #22

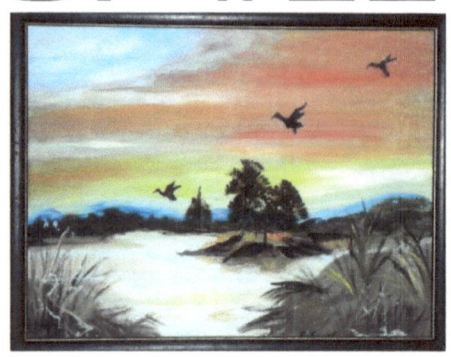

SP #23

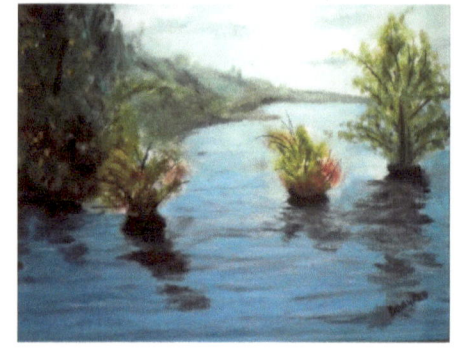

SP #24

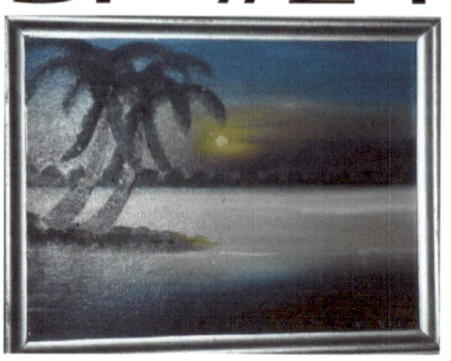

SP #25

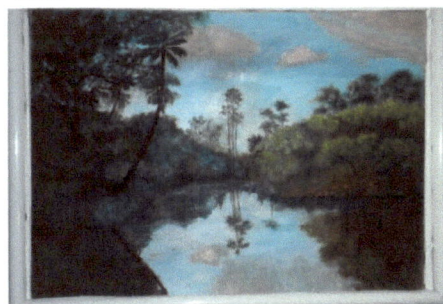

SP #26

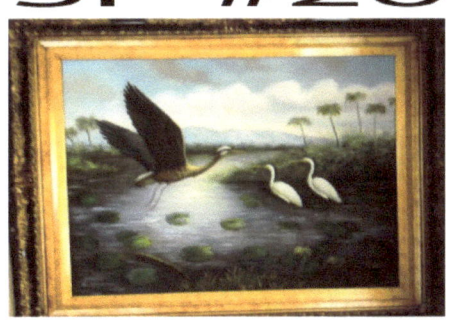

SP #27

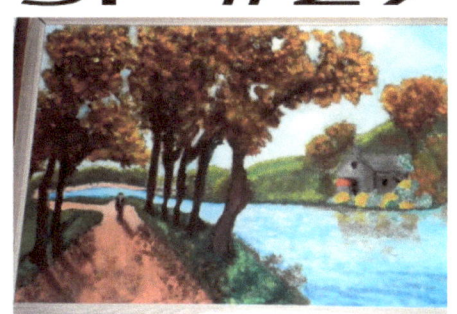

SP #28

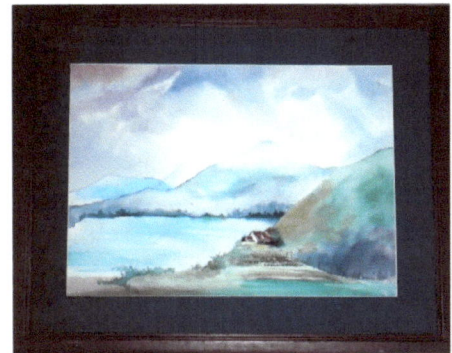

SP #29

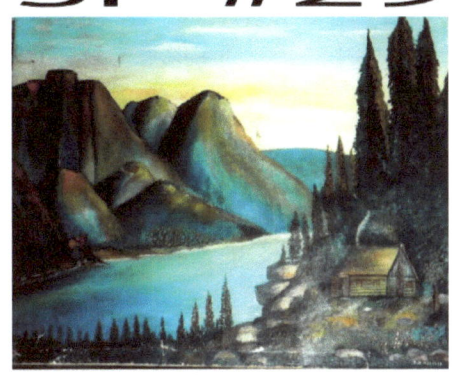

SP #30

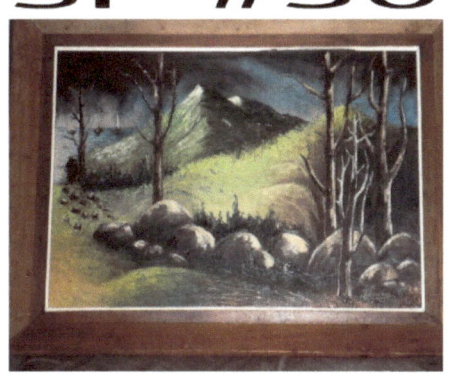

SP #31

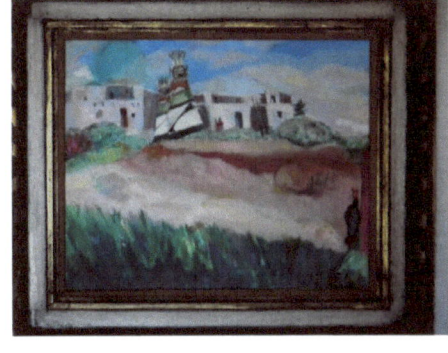

SP #32

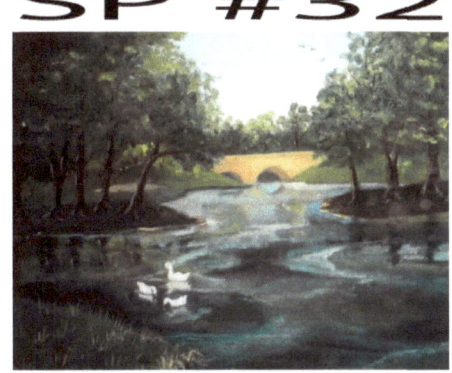

SP #33

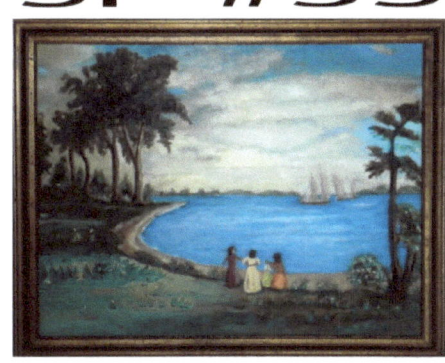

SP #34

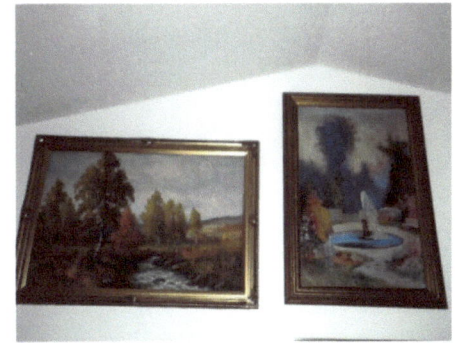

SP #35

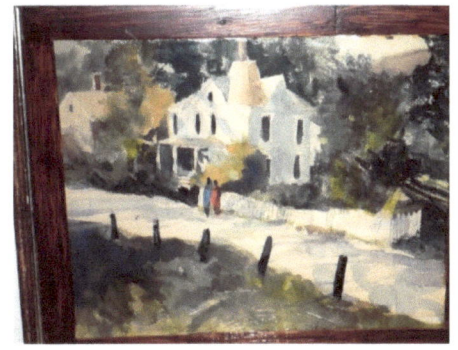

SP #36

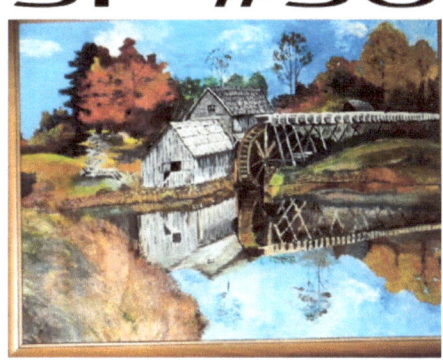

SP #37

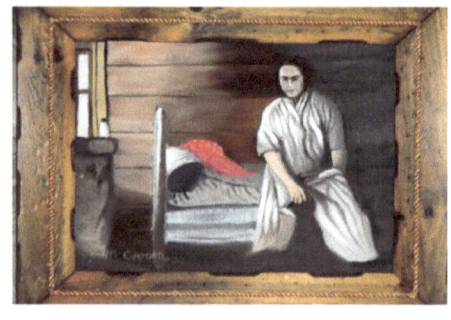

SP #38

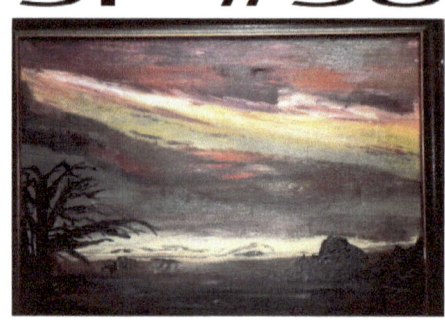

SP #39

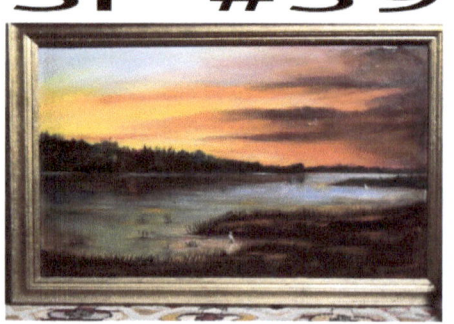

SP #40

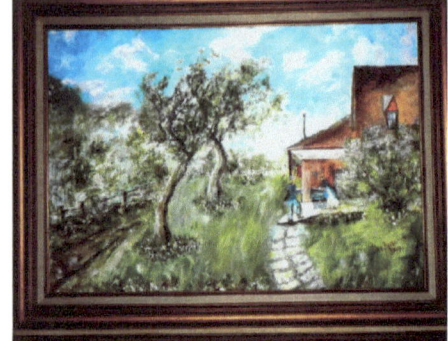

SP #41

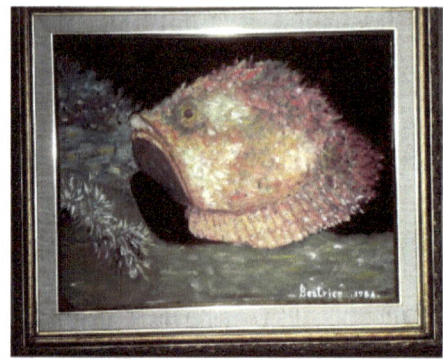

SP #42

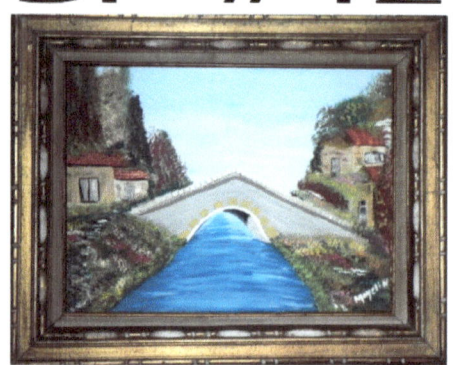

SP #43

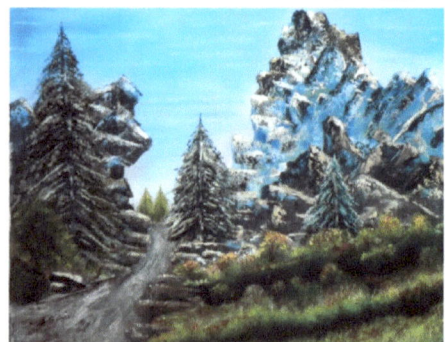

SP #44

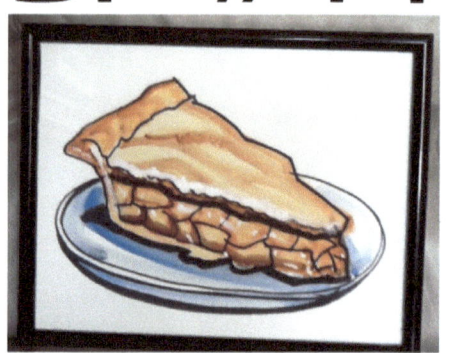

SP #45

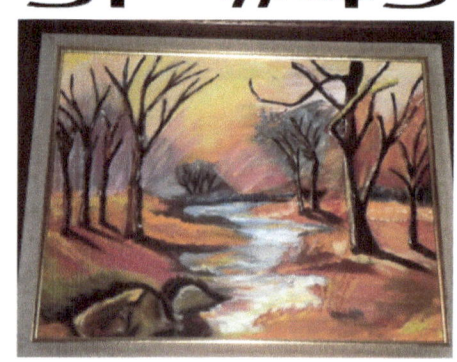

SP #46

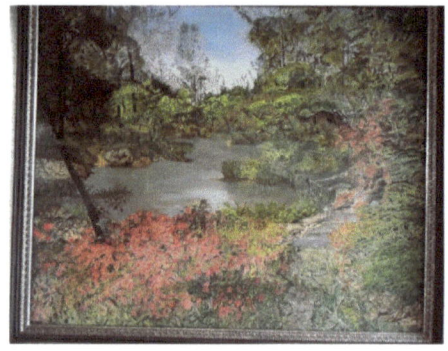

SP #47

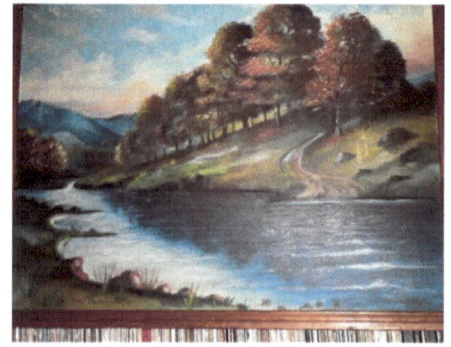

SP #48

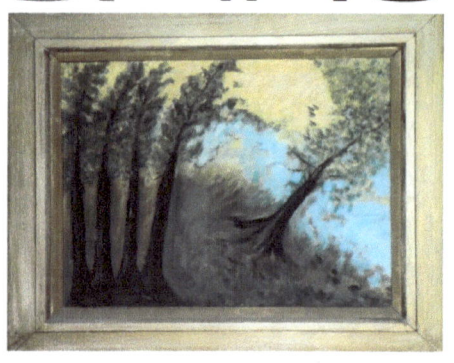

SP #49

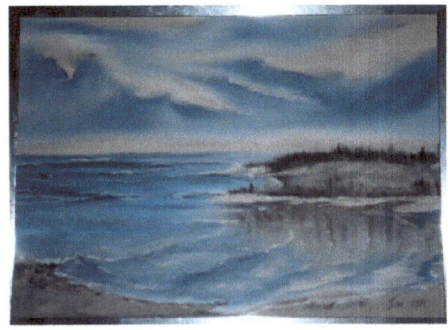

SP #50

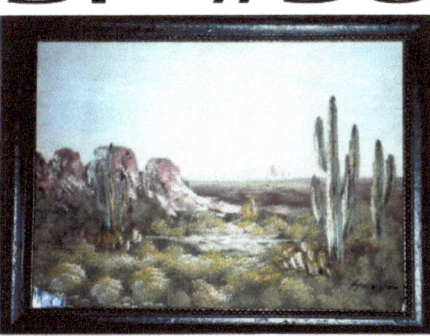

SP #51

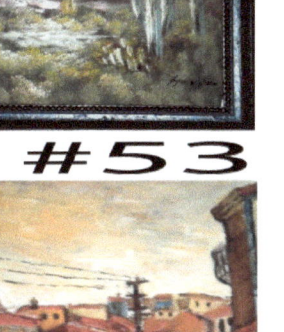

SP #52

SP #53

SP #54

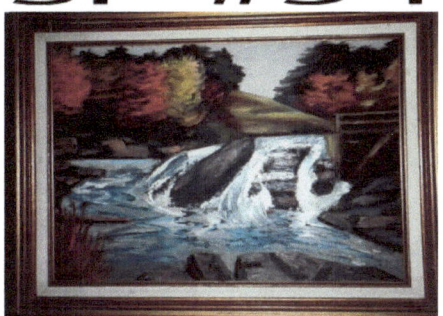

SP #55

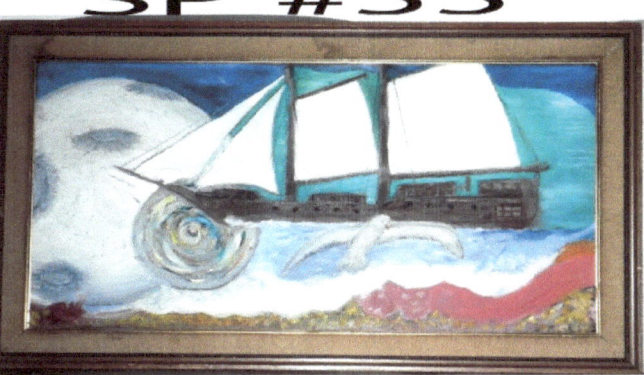

SP #56

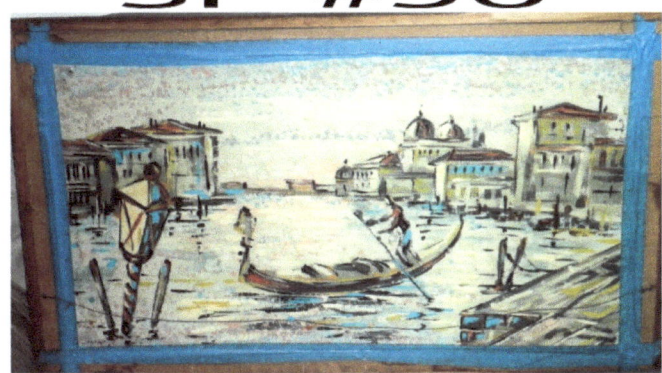

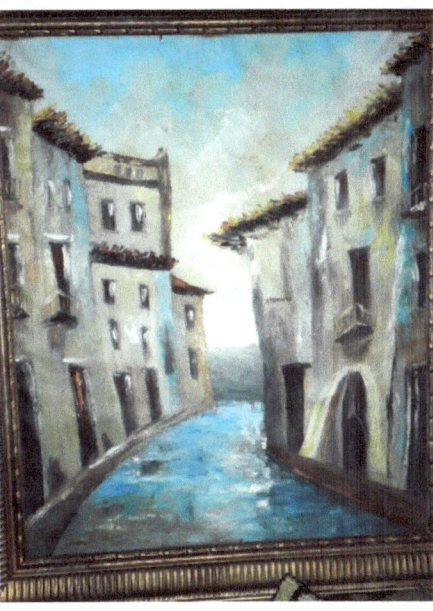

SP #57

SP #58

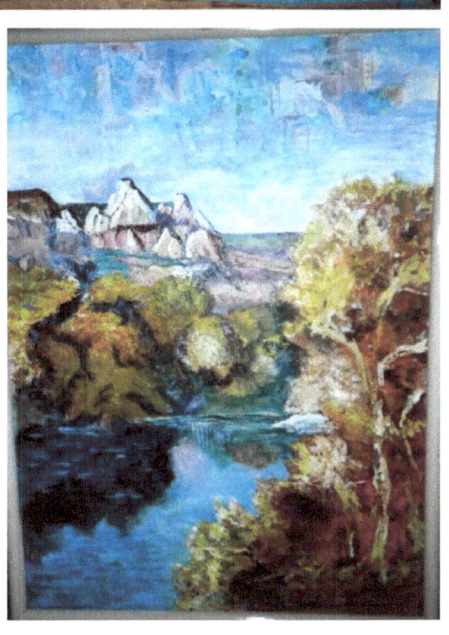

SP #59
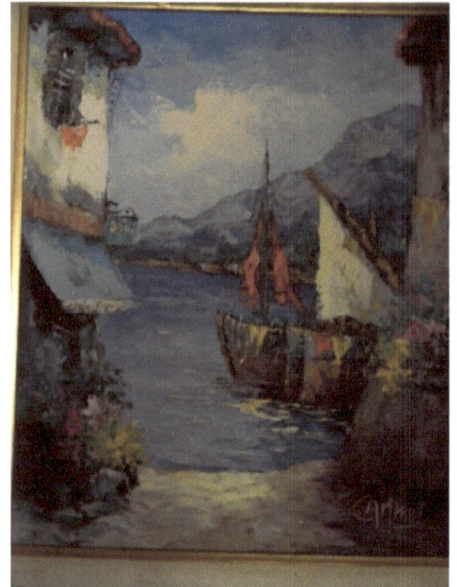

SP #60
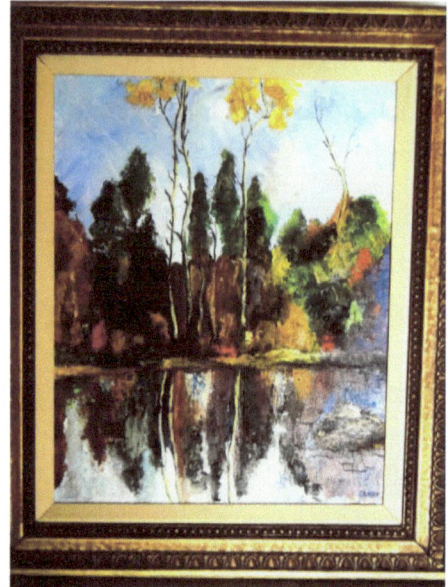

SP #61
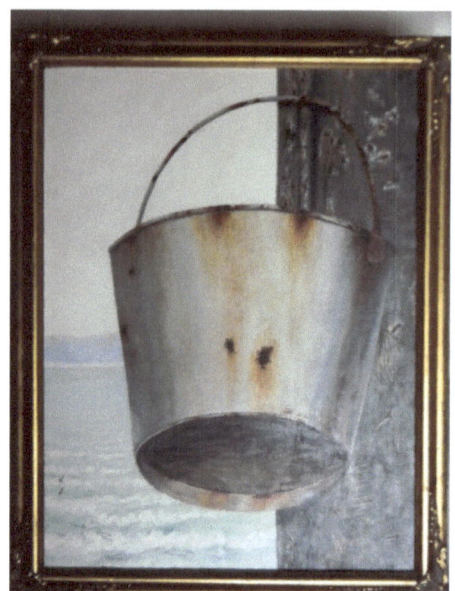

SP #62
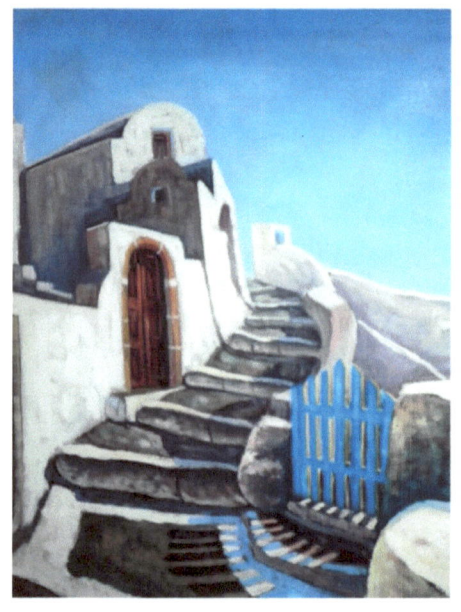

SP #63
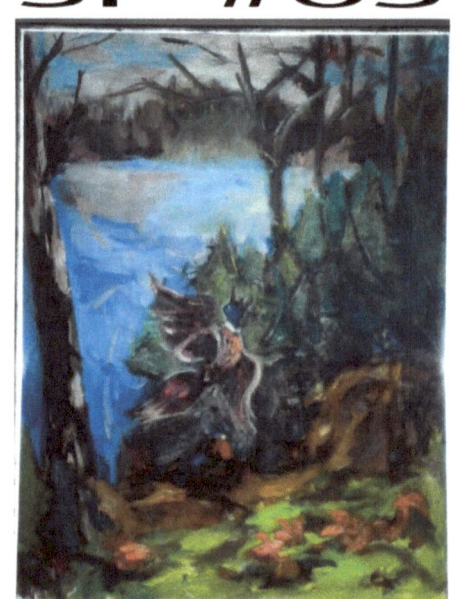

SP #64
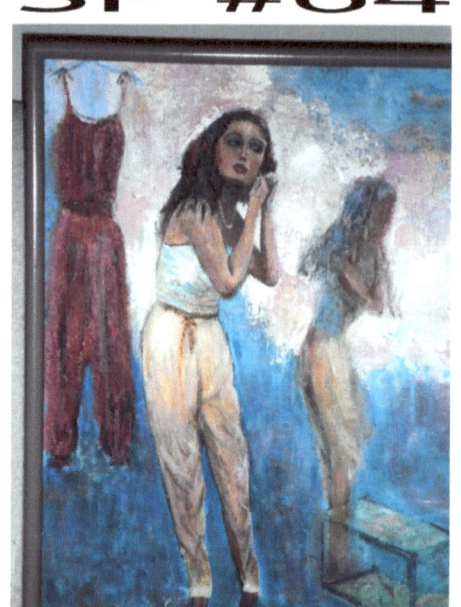

SP #65
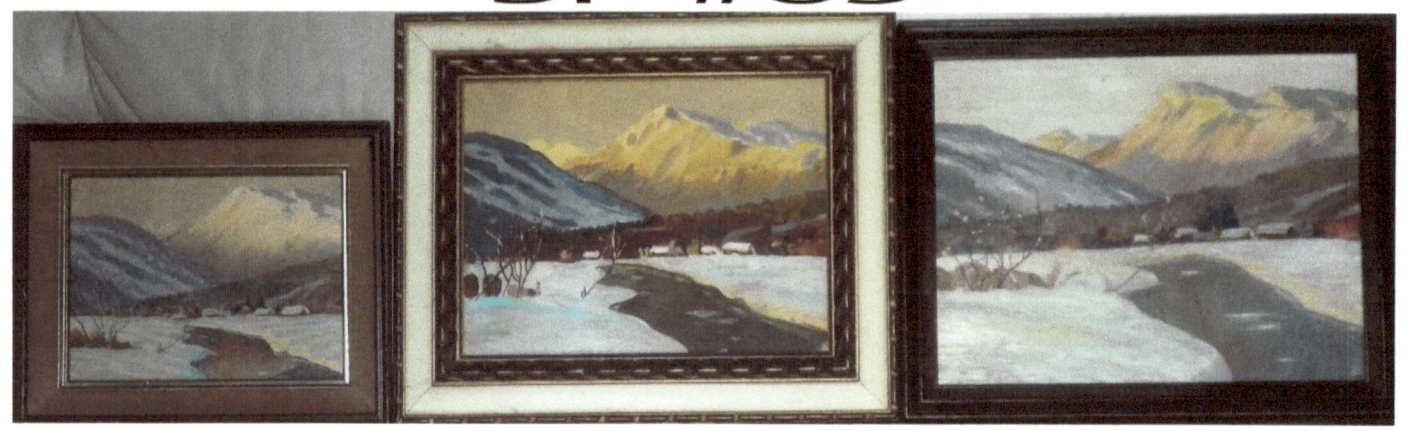

SP #66 SP #67 SP #68

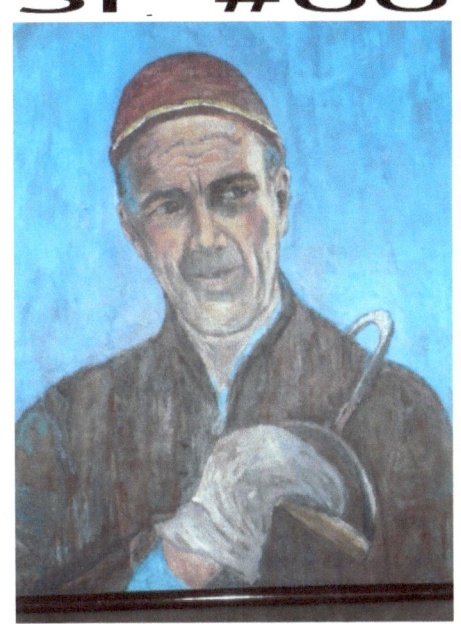 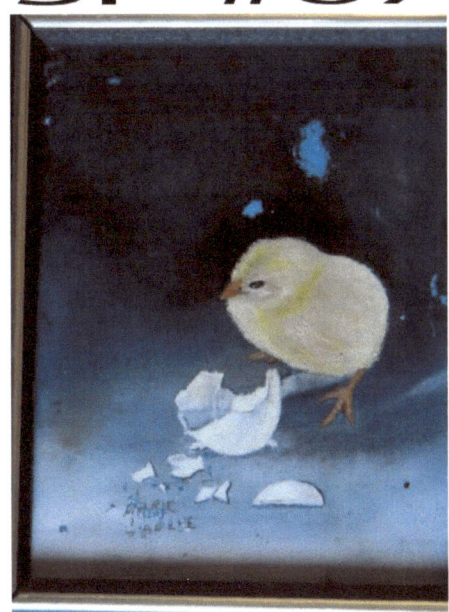 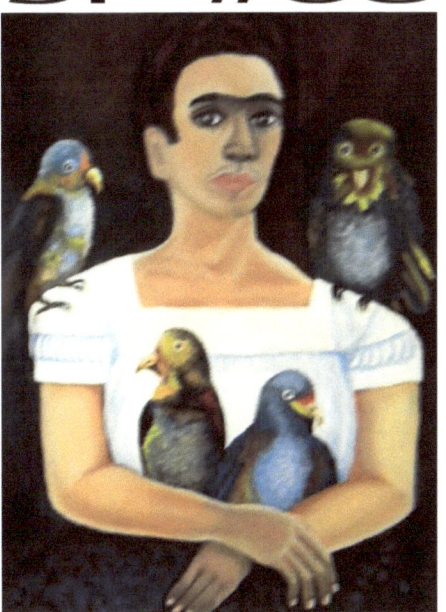

SP #69 SP #70 SP #71

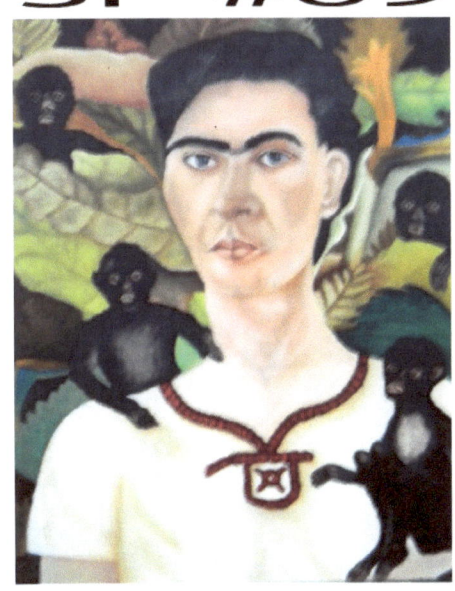 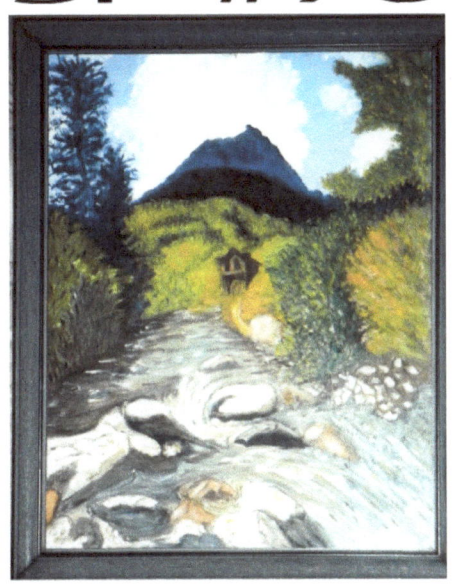 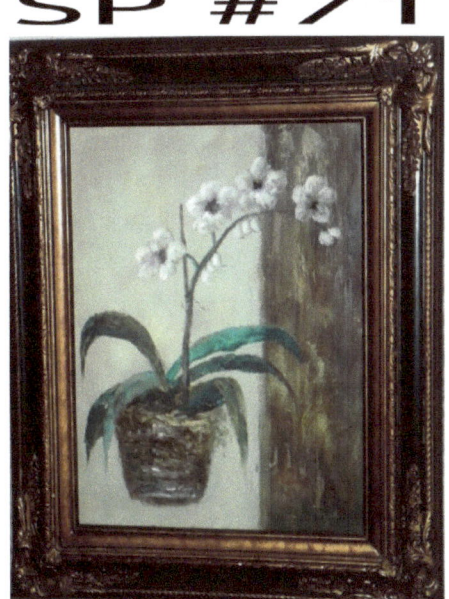

SP #72

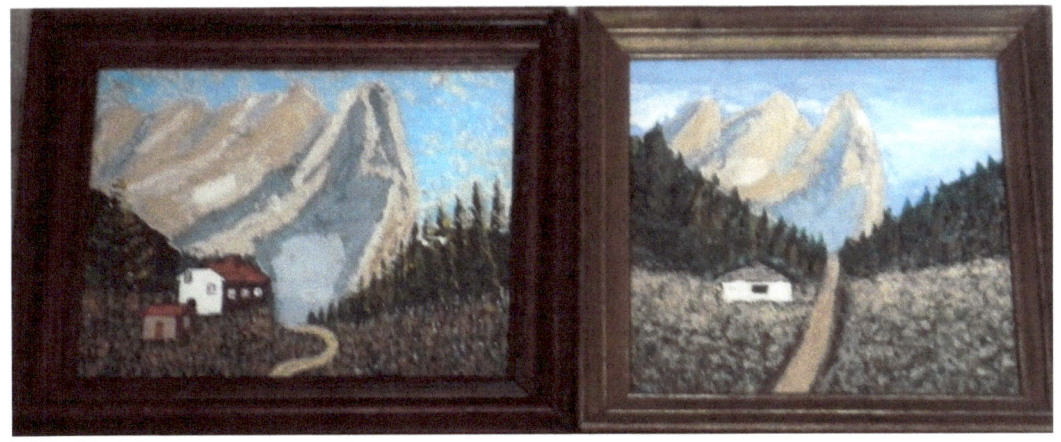

SP #73
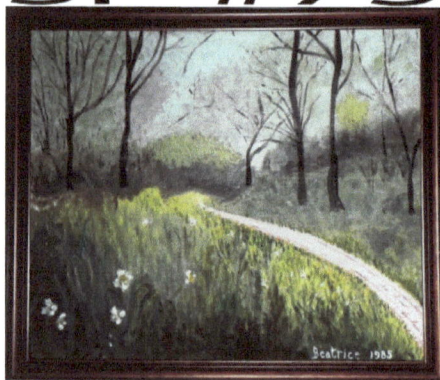

SP #74
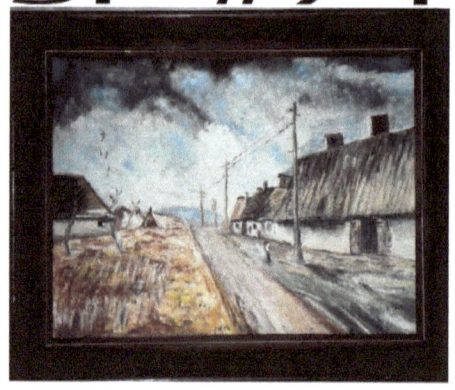

SP #75
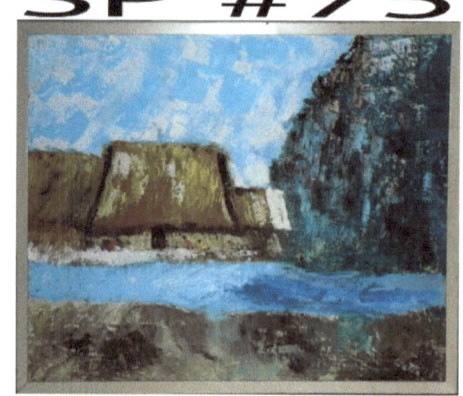

SP #76
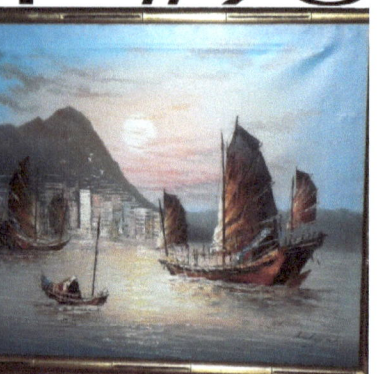

SP #77
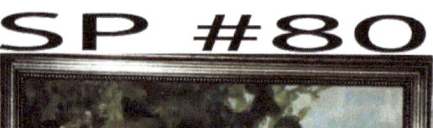
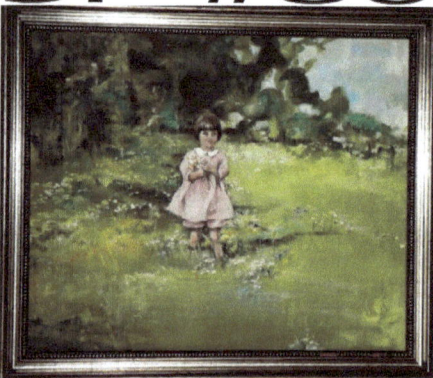

SP #78
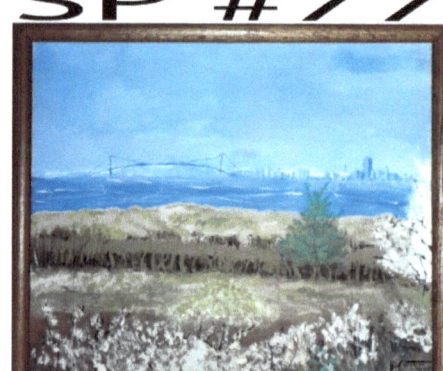

SP #79
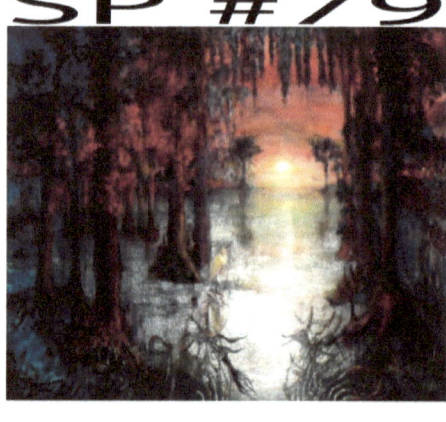

SP #80
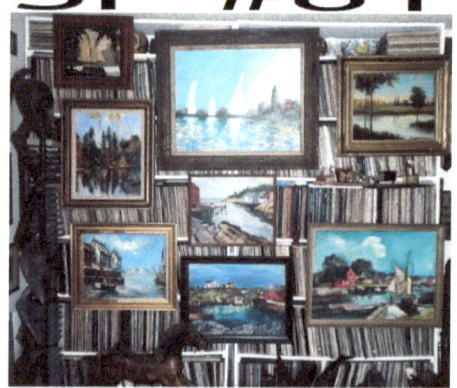

SP #81

SP #82
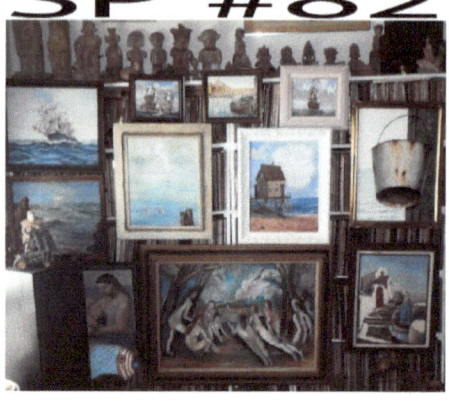

SP #83
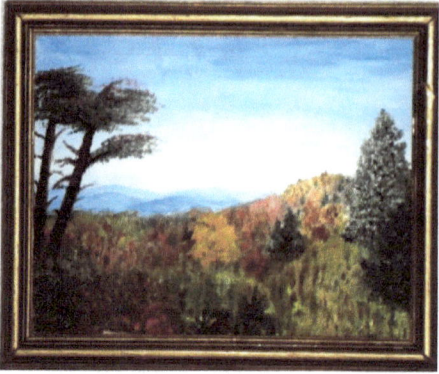

SP #84
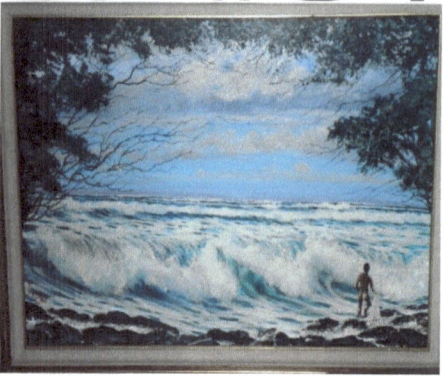

SP #85

SP #86

SP #87

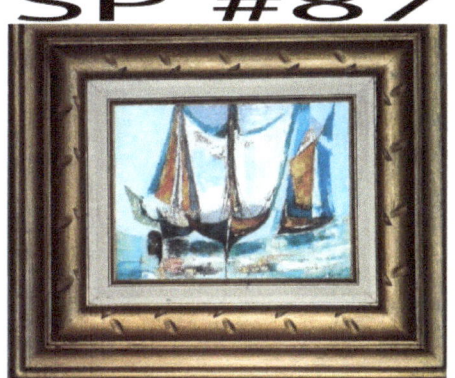

SP #88

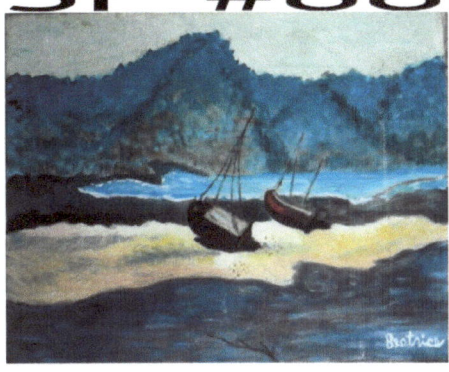

SP #89

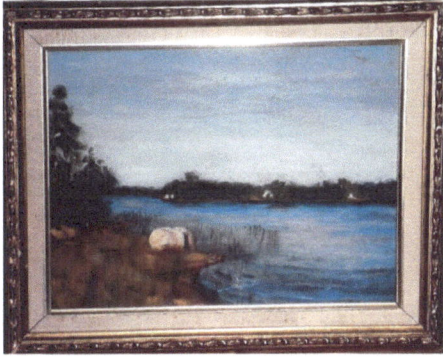

SP #90

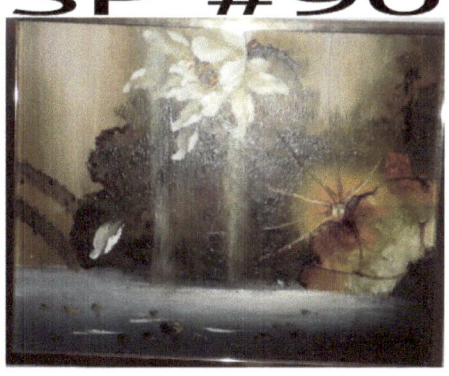

SP #91

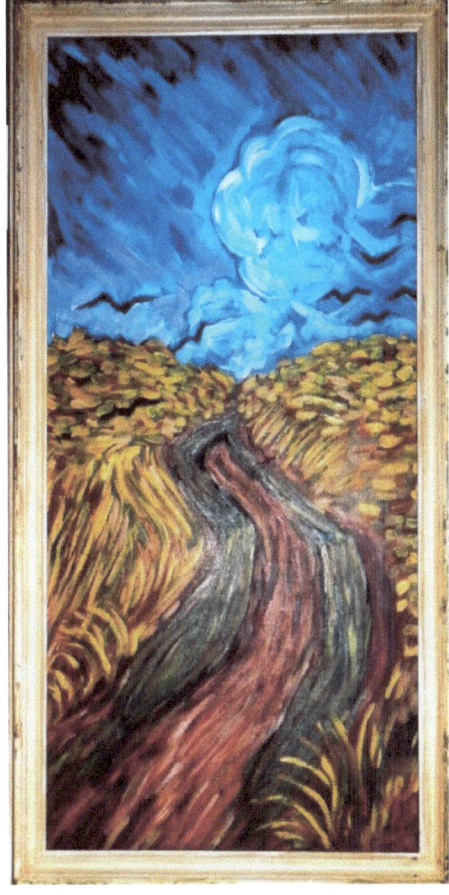

SP #92

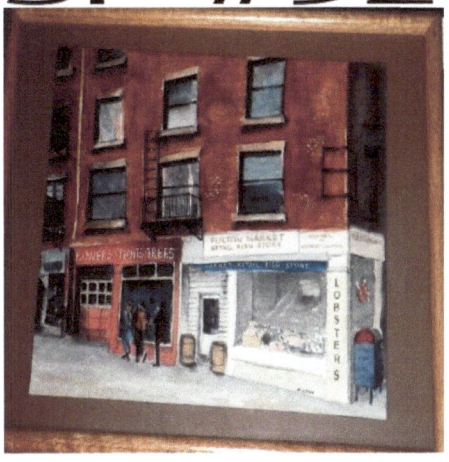

SP #93

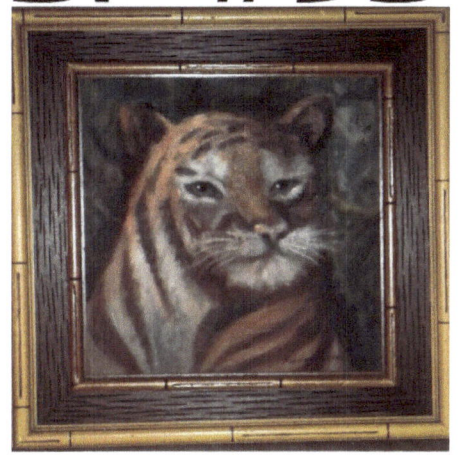

SP #94

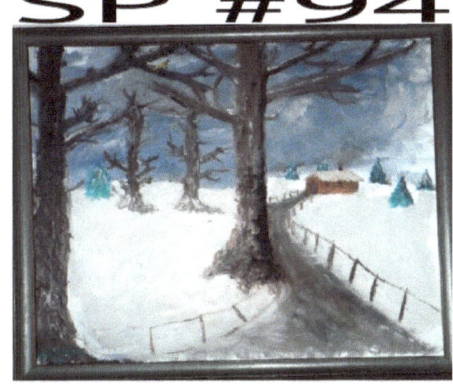

SP #95

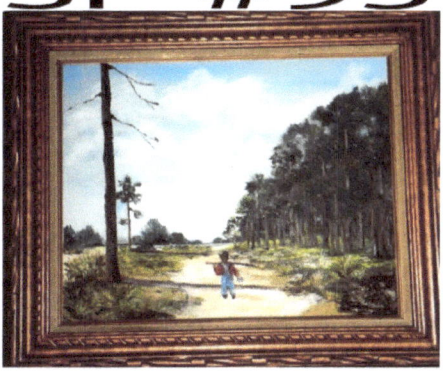

SP #96

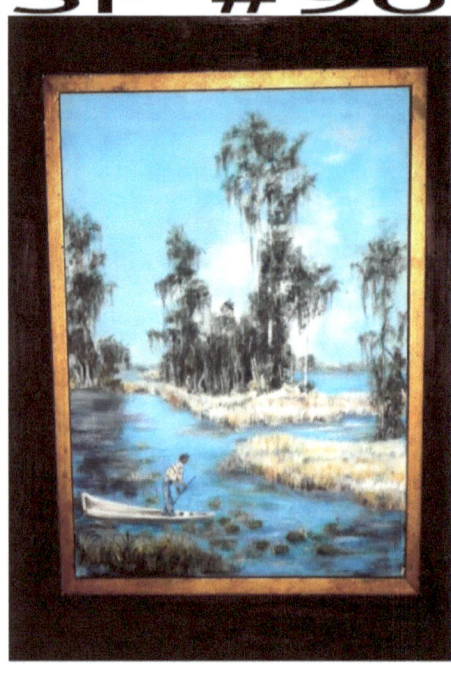

SP #97

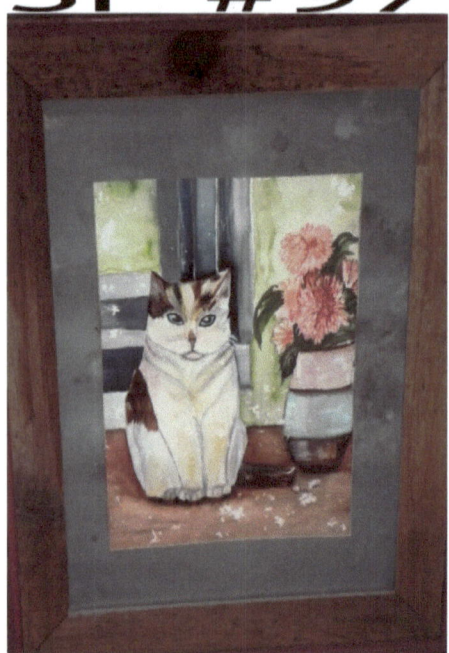

SP #98

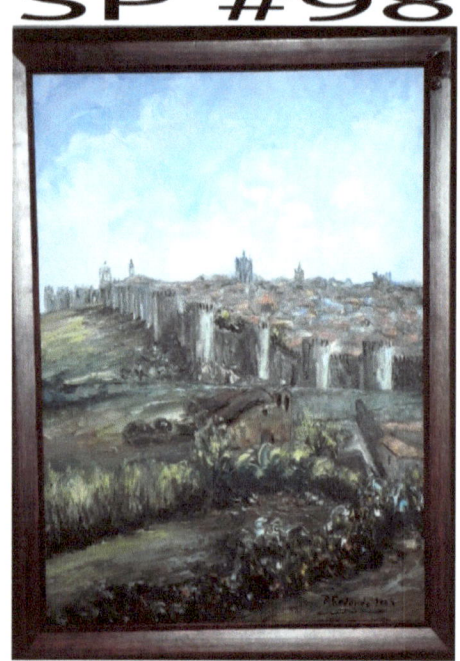

SP #99

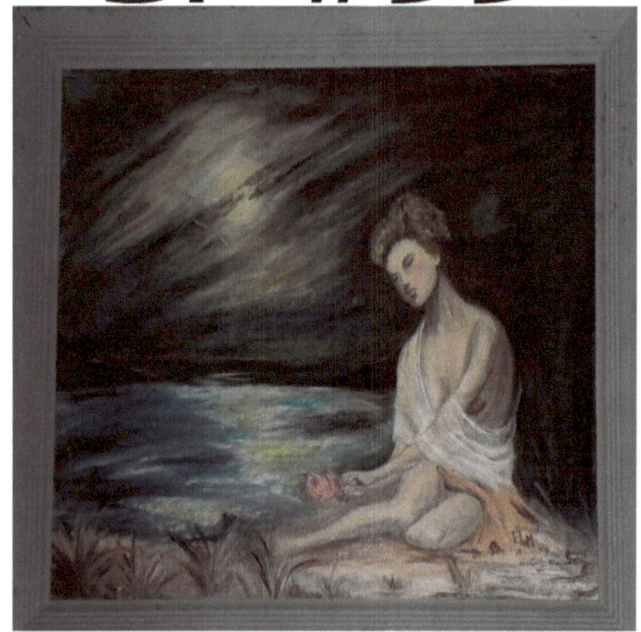

SP #100

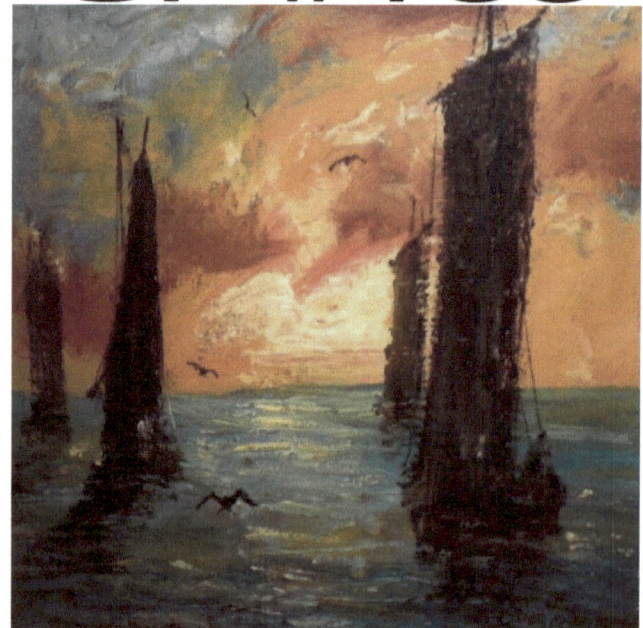

A Gallery of Selected Enlargements

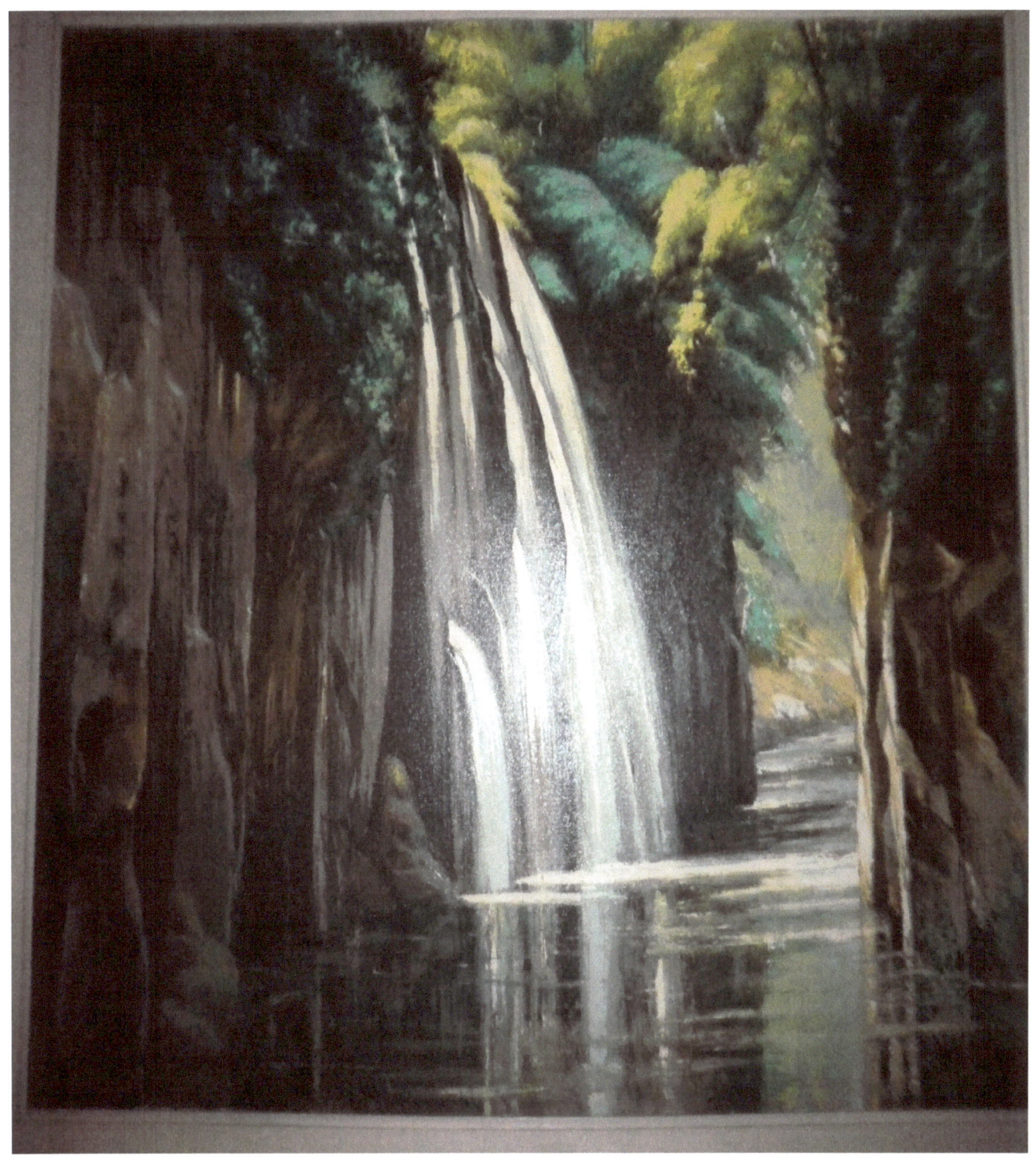

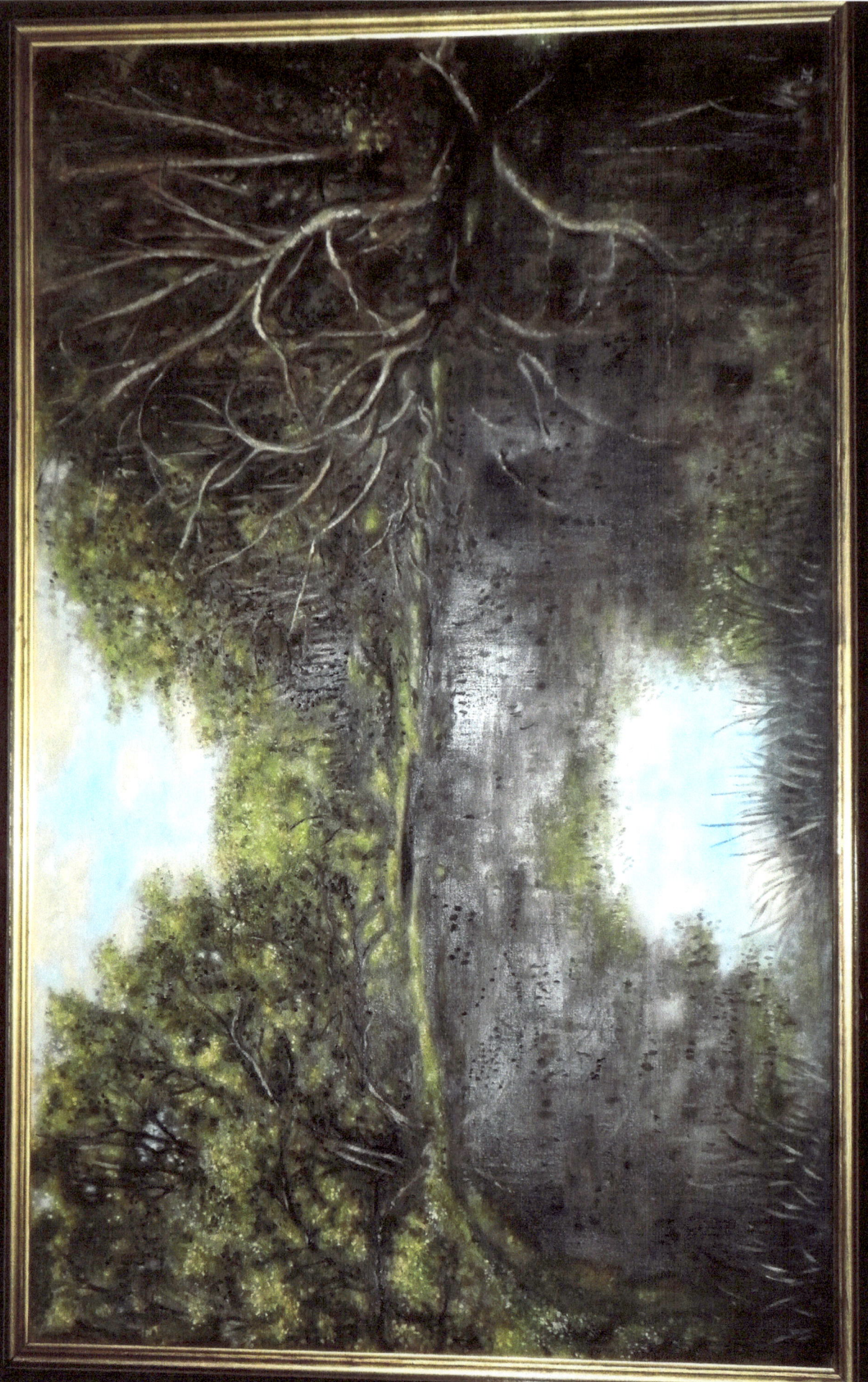

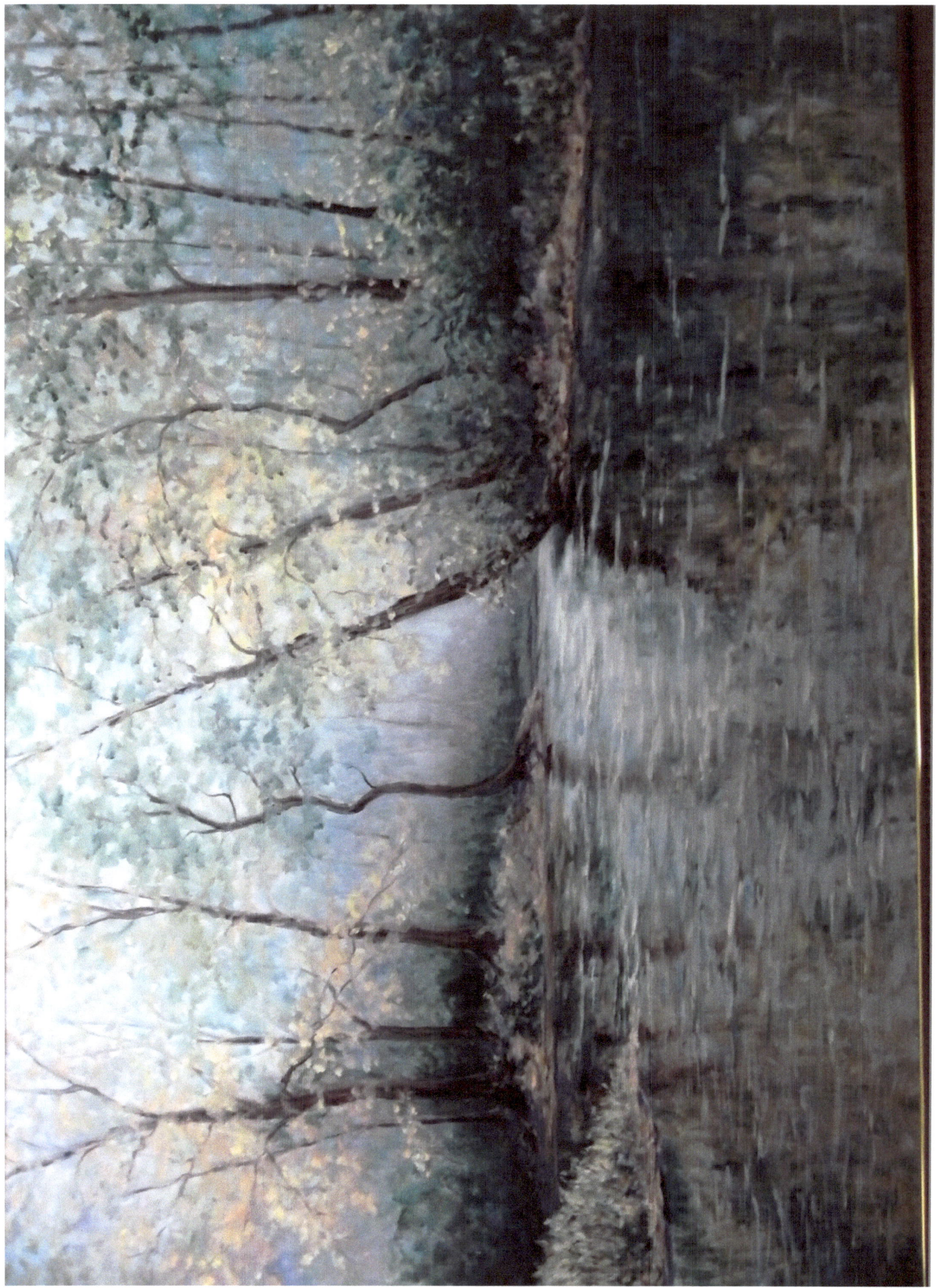

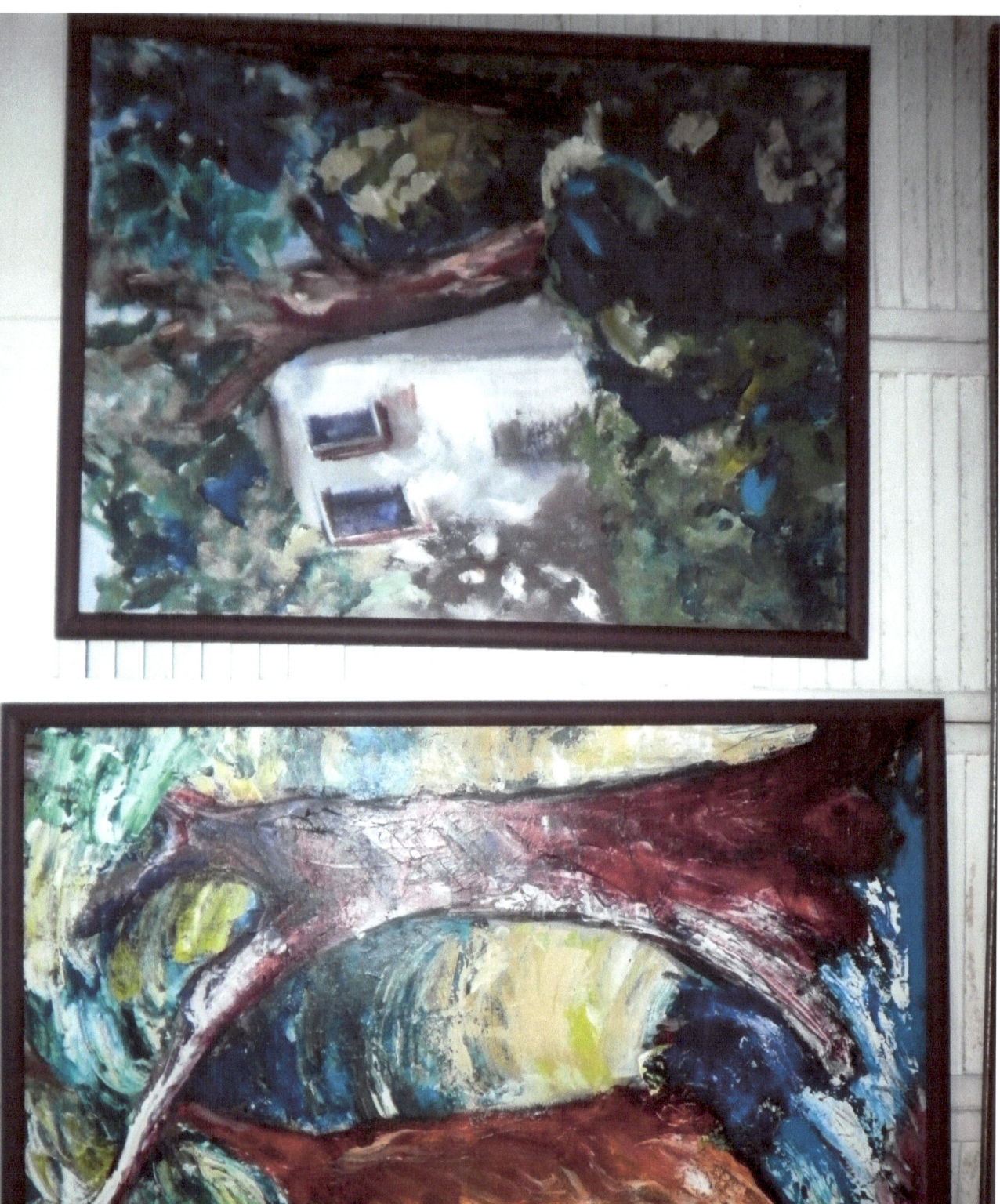

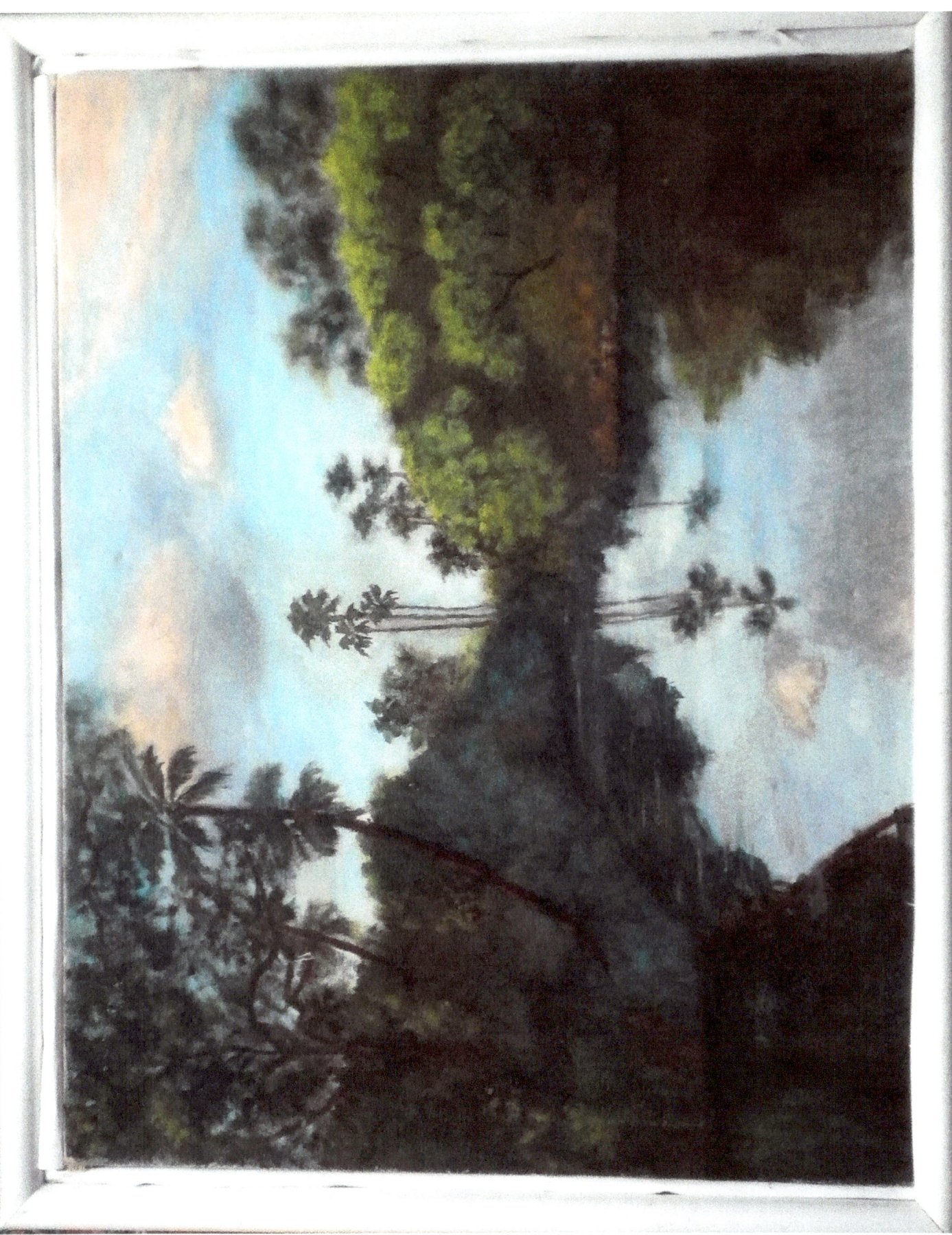

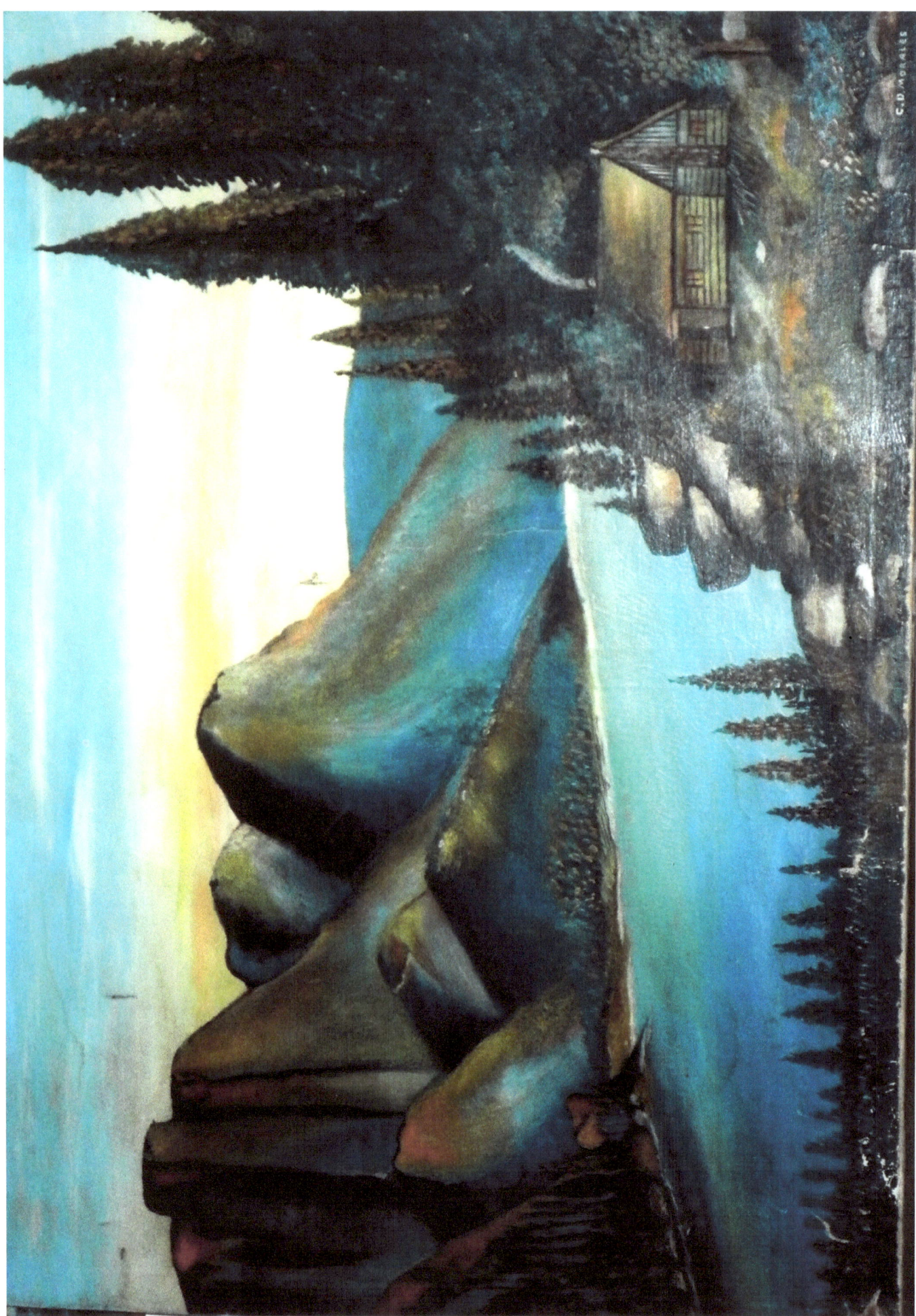

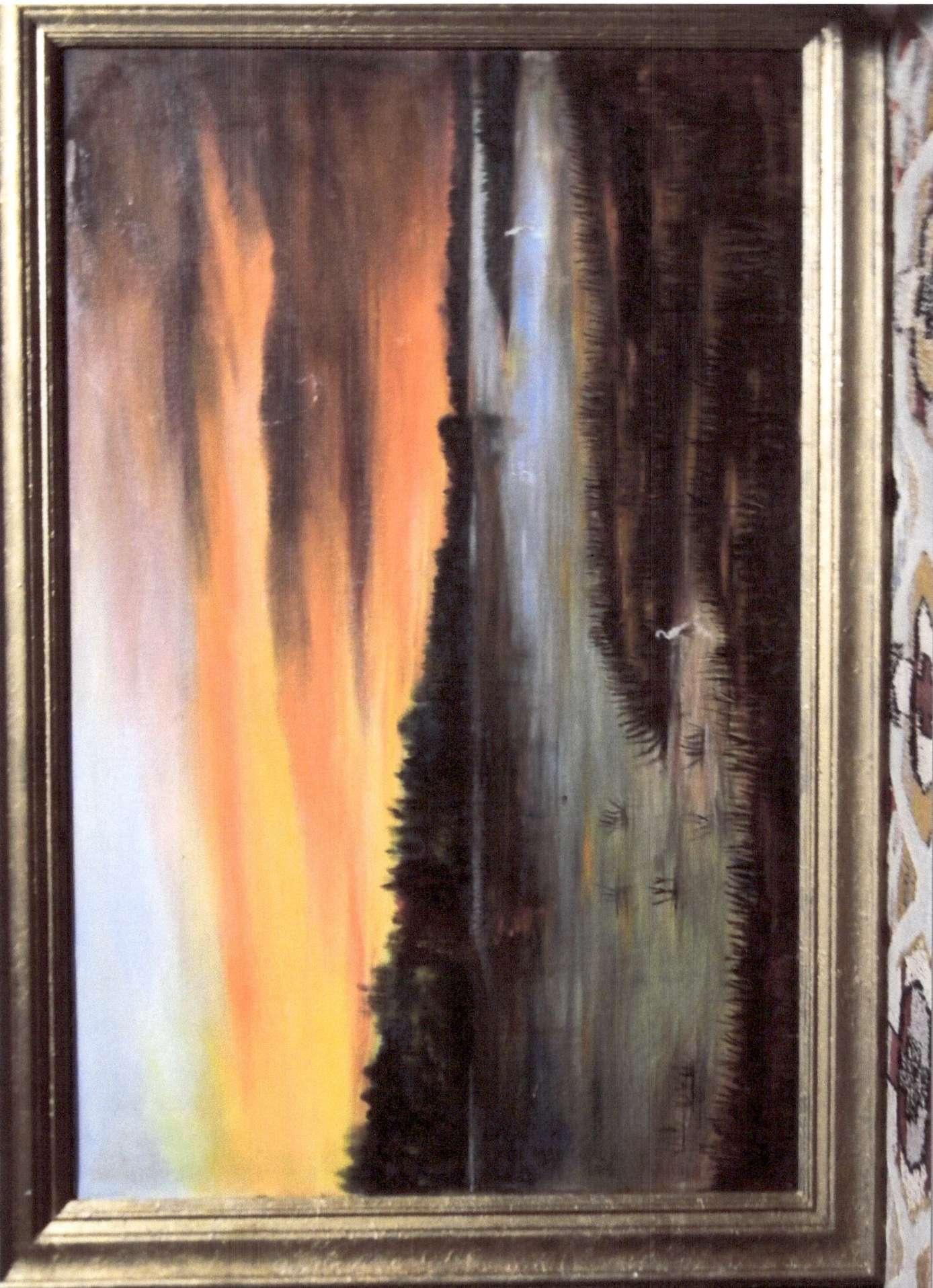

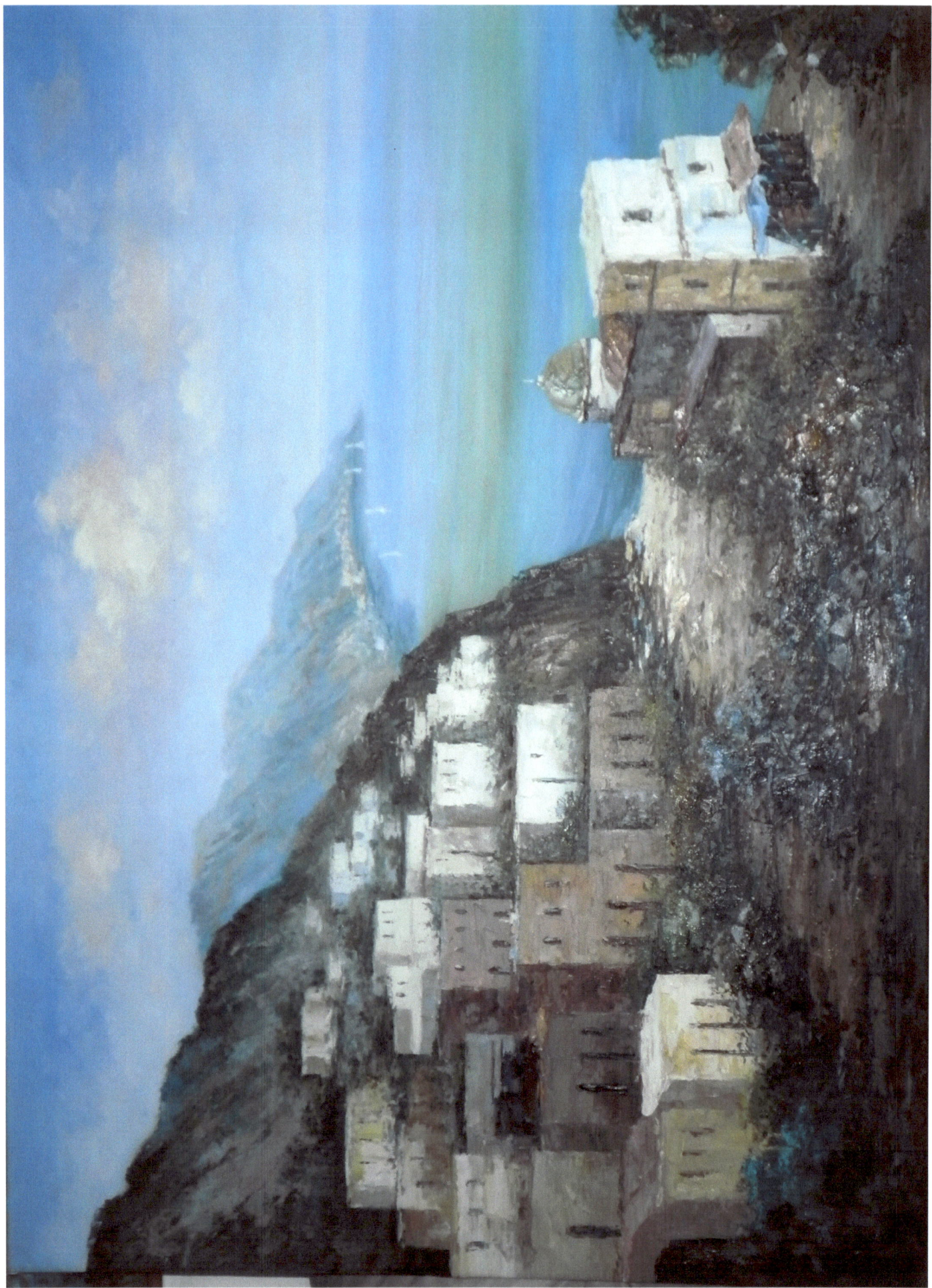

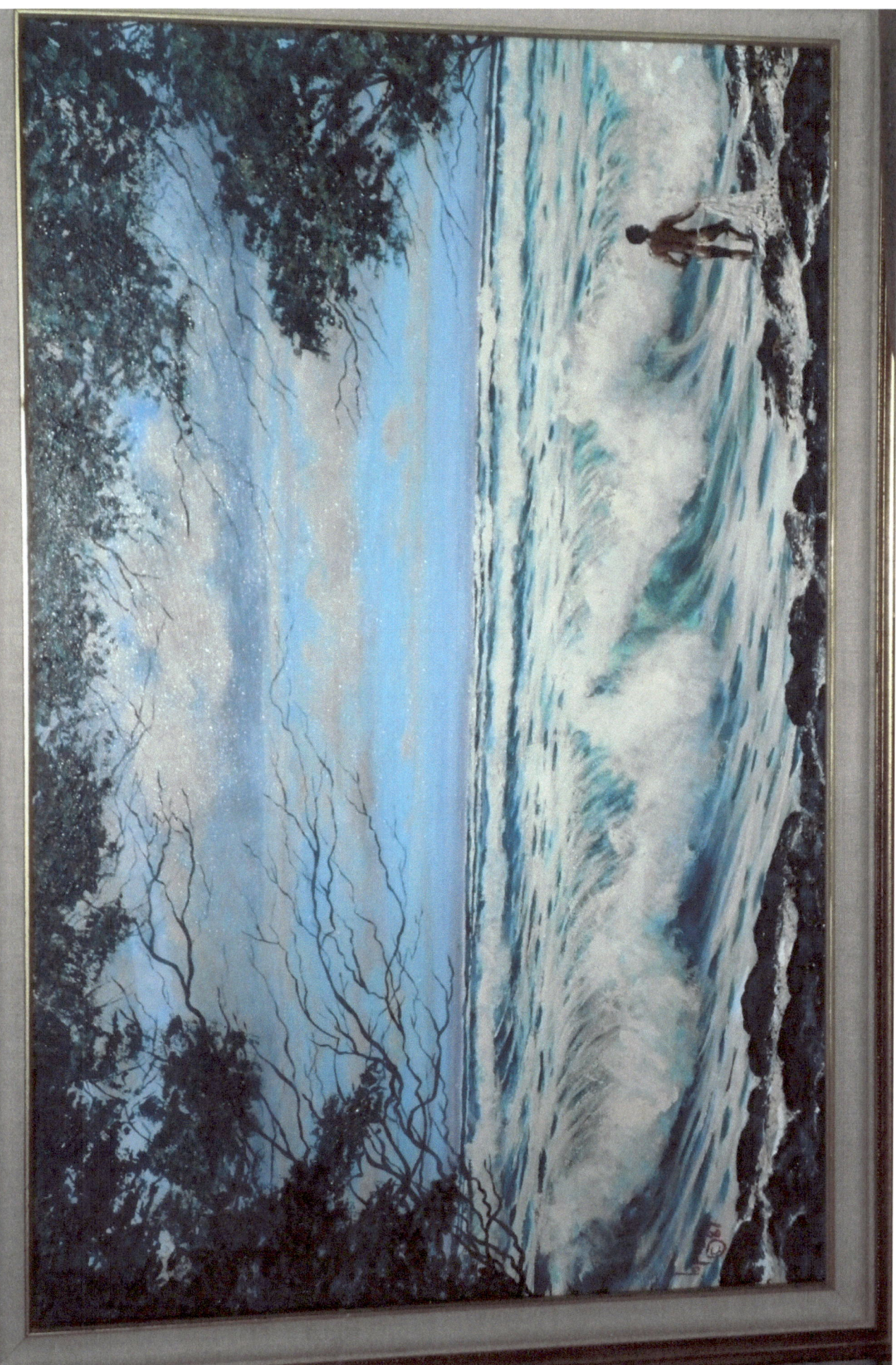

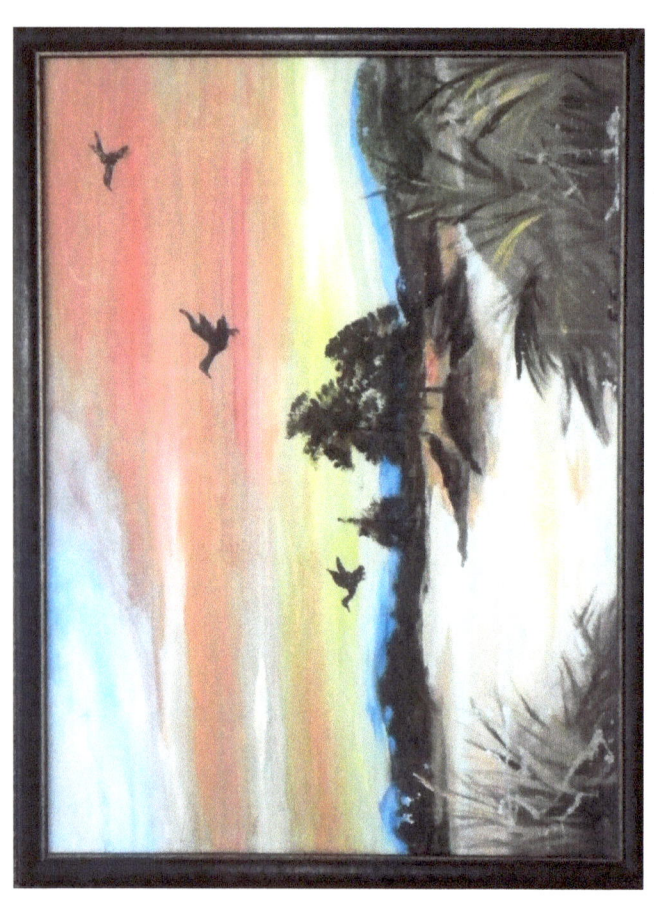

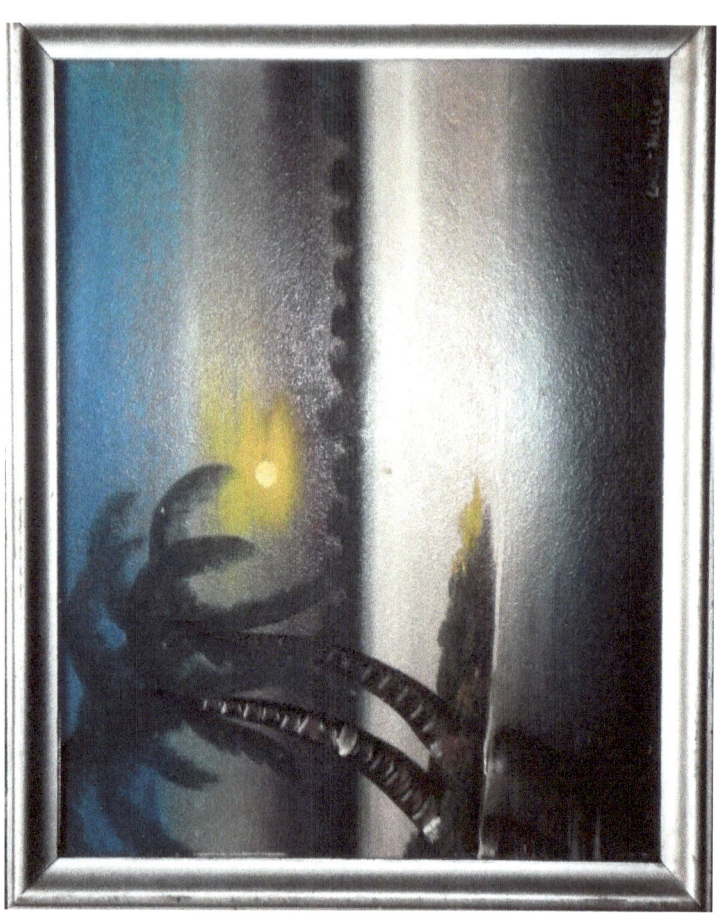

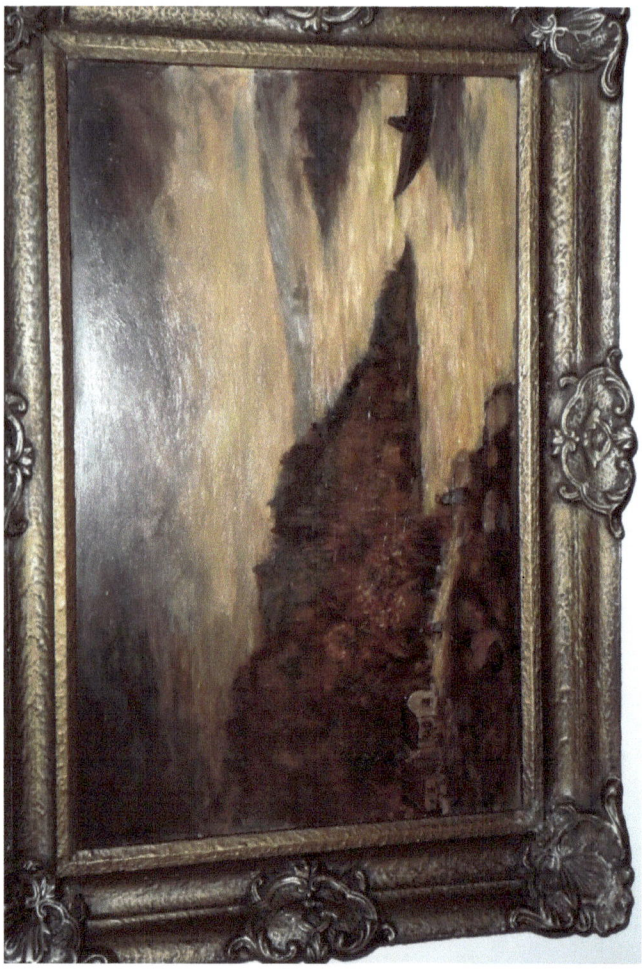

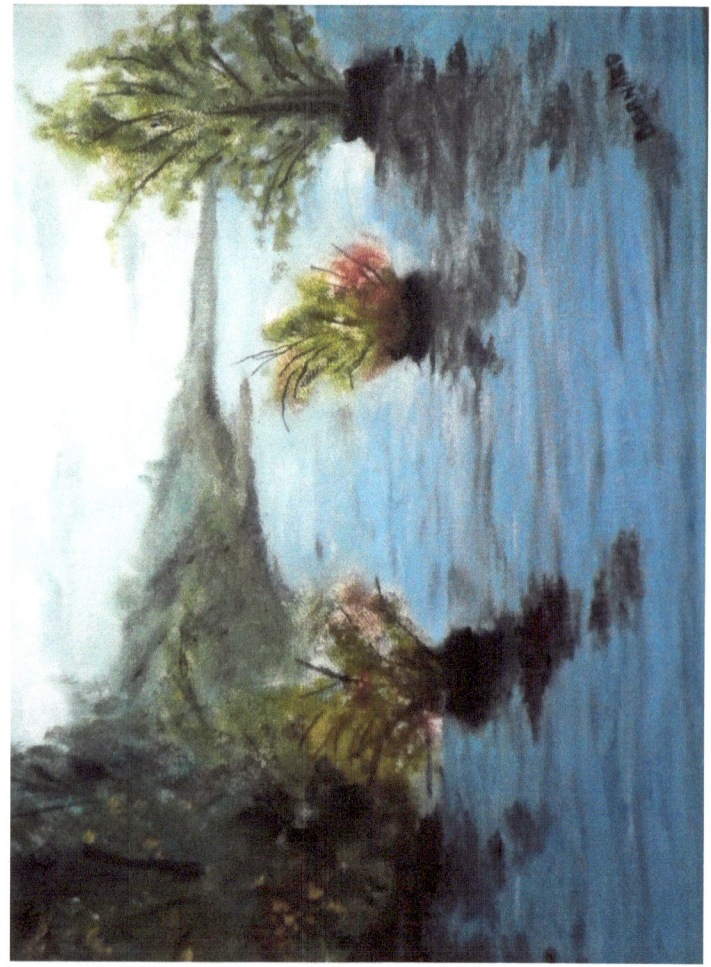

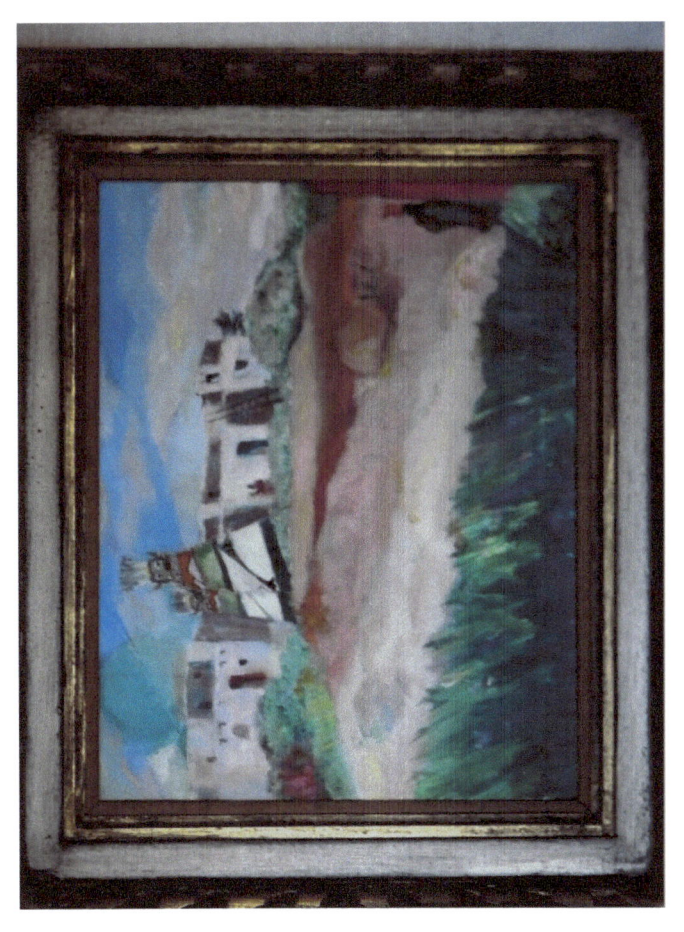
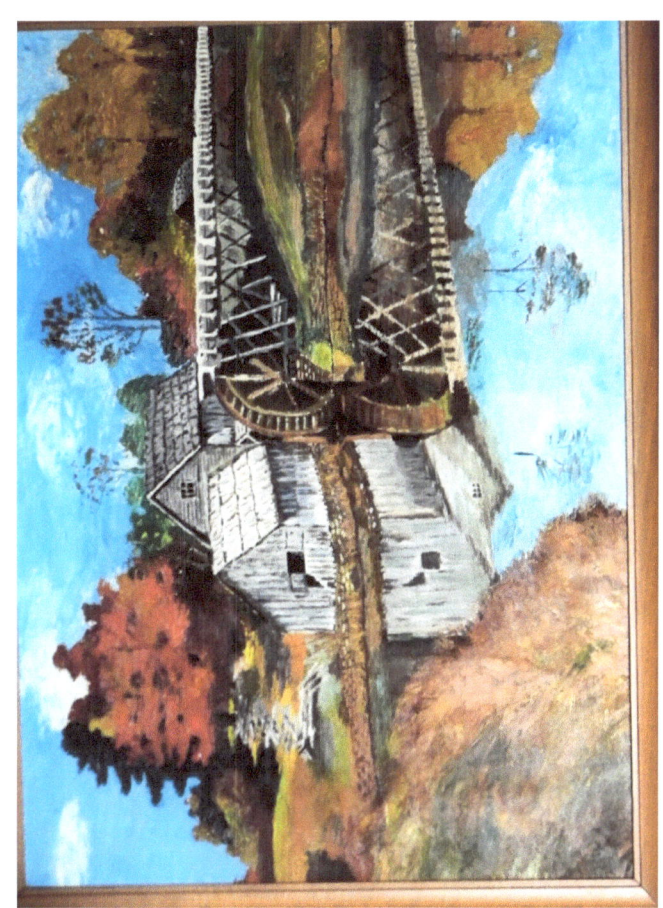
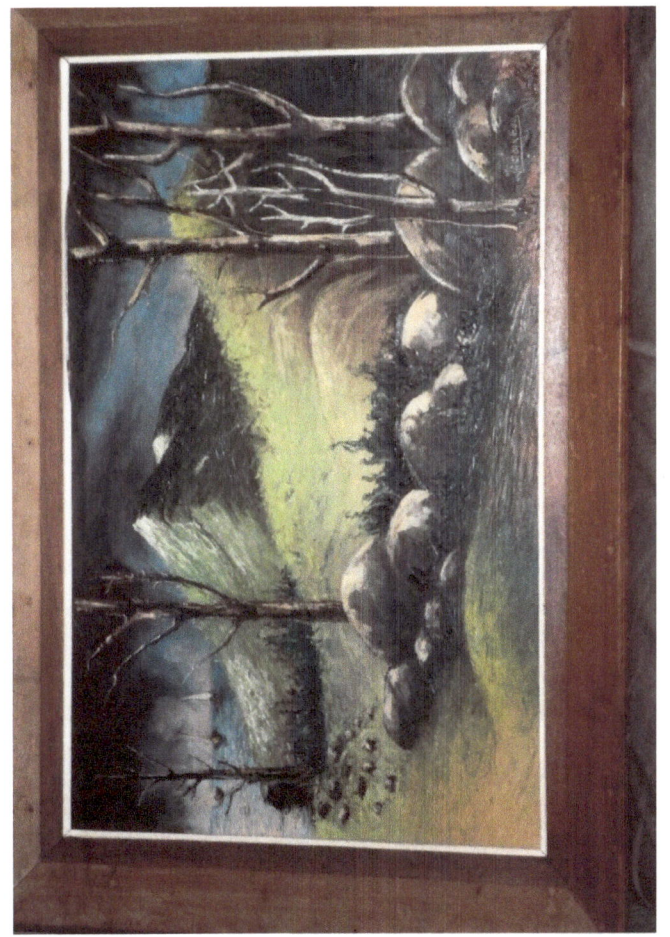
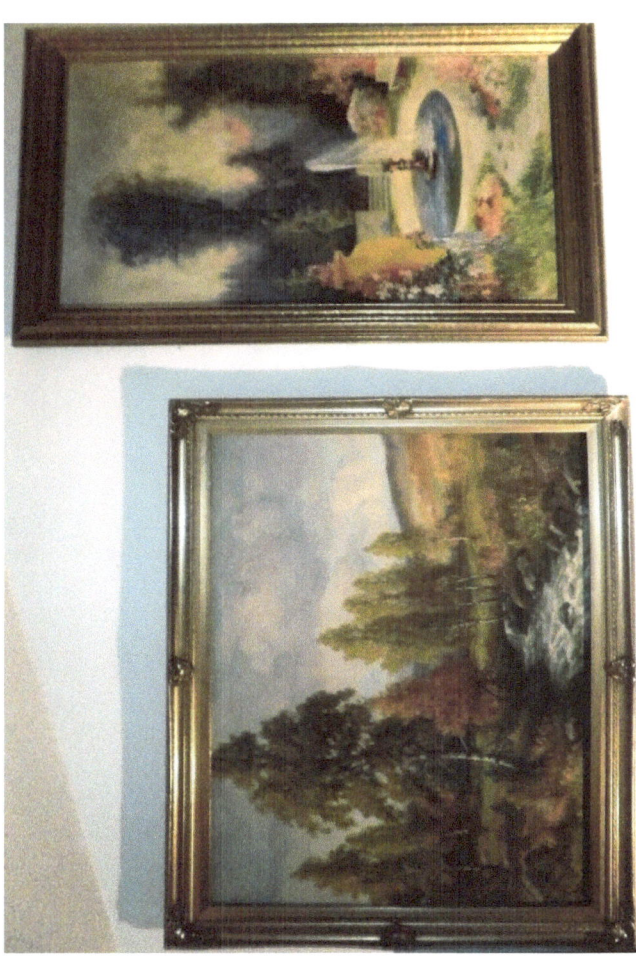

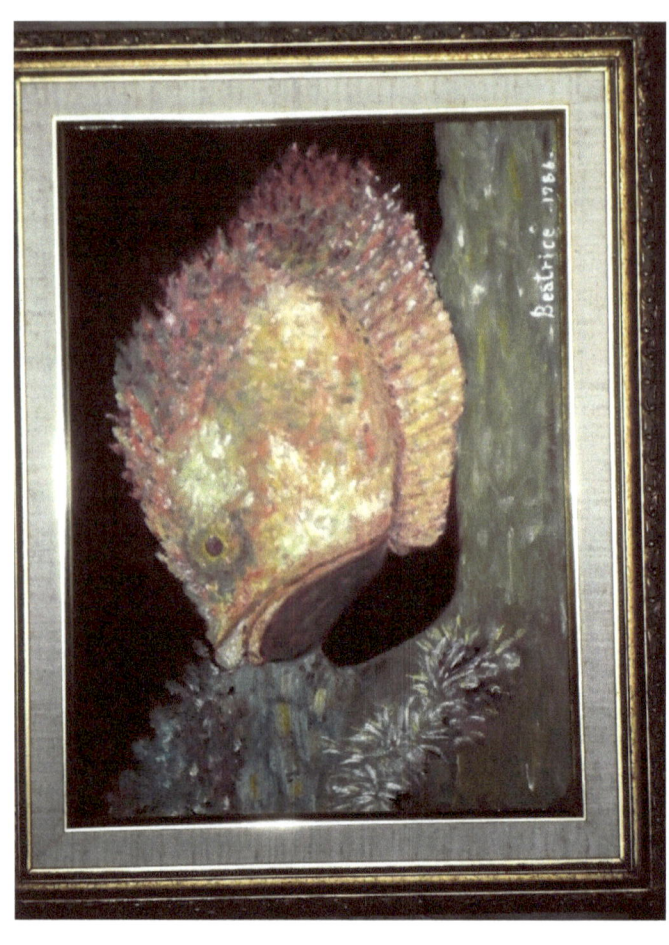

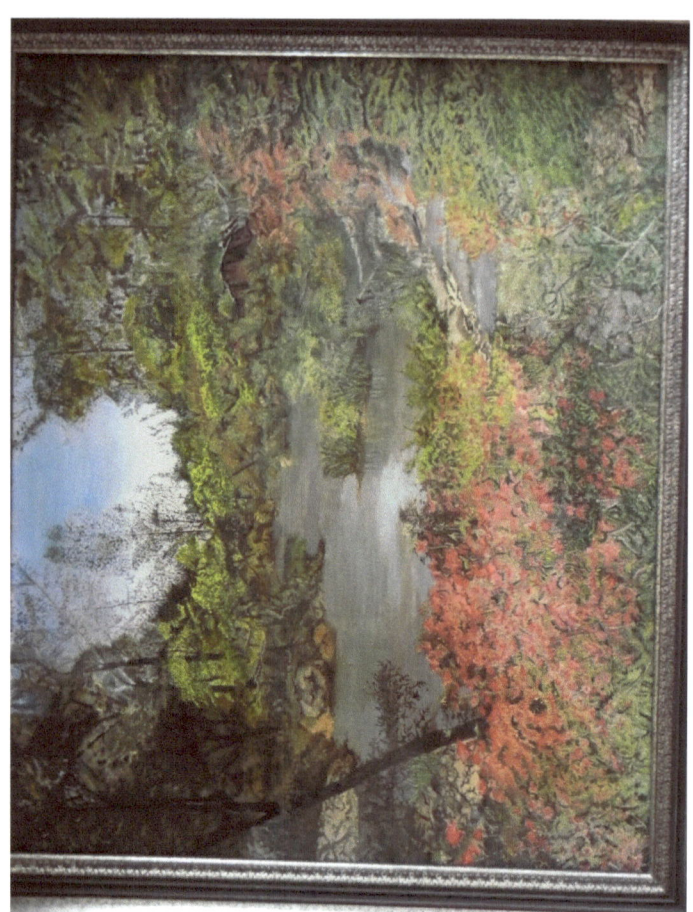

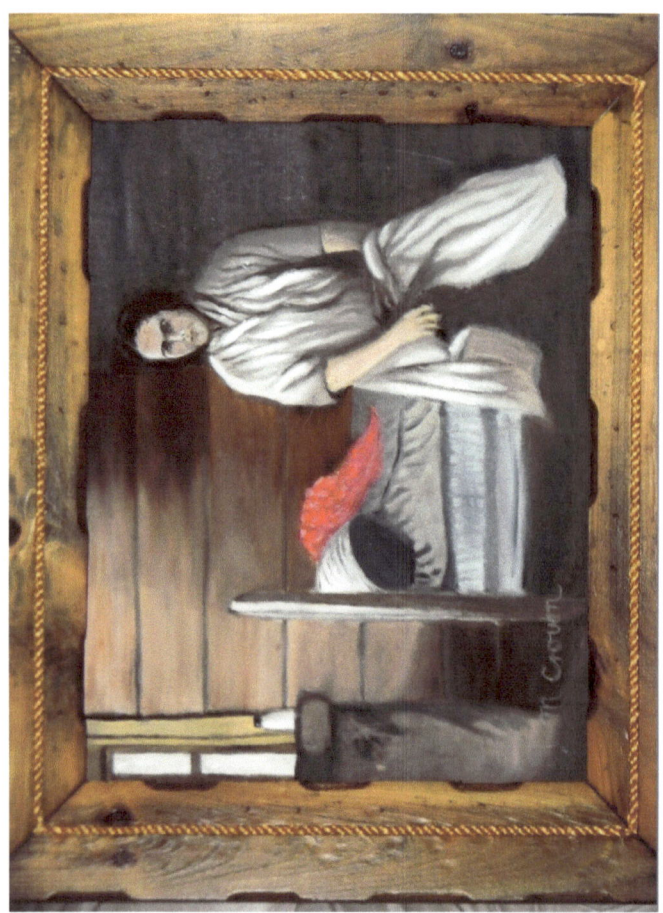

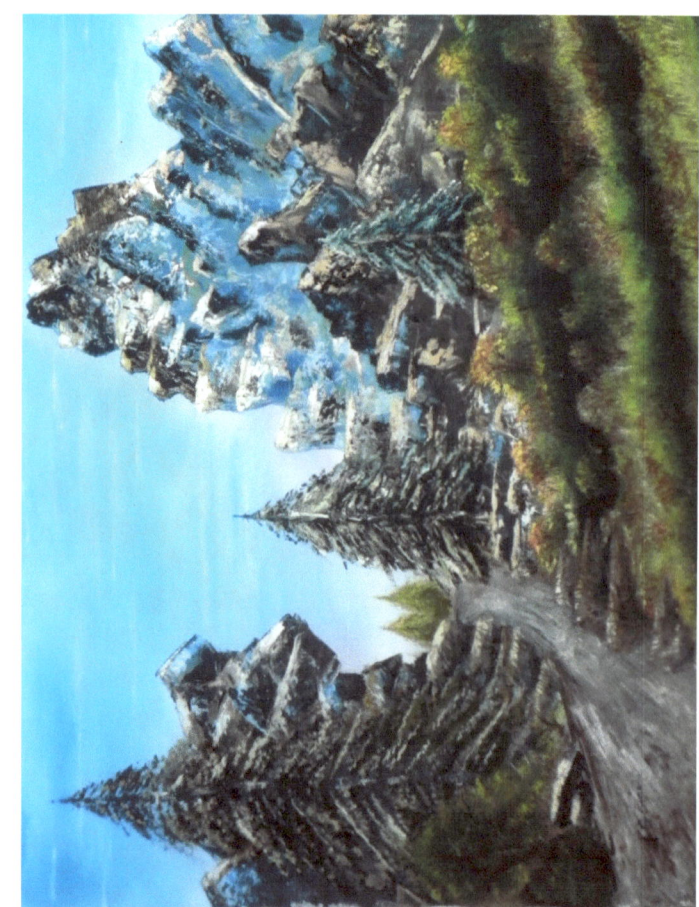

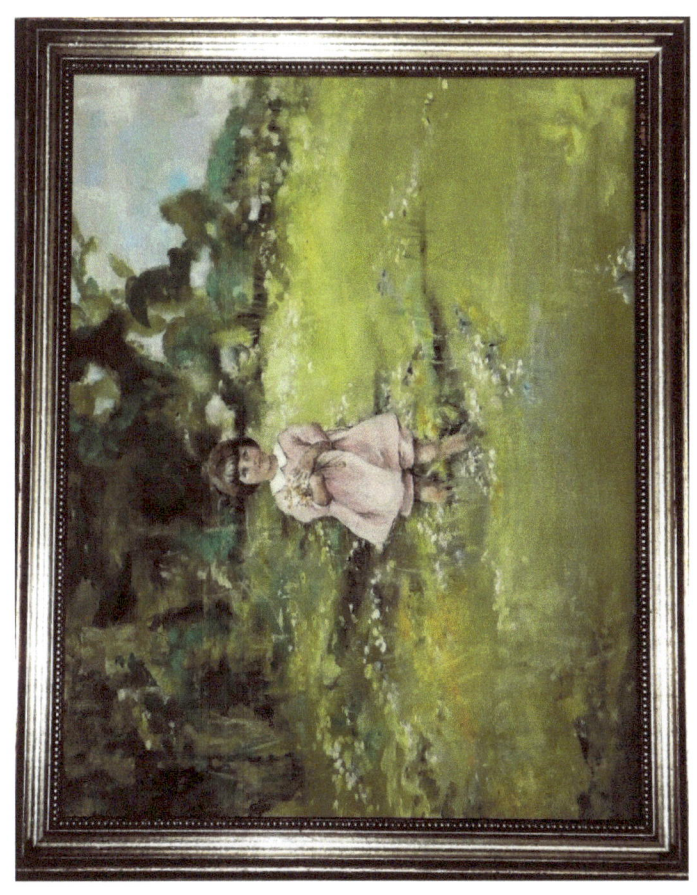

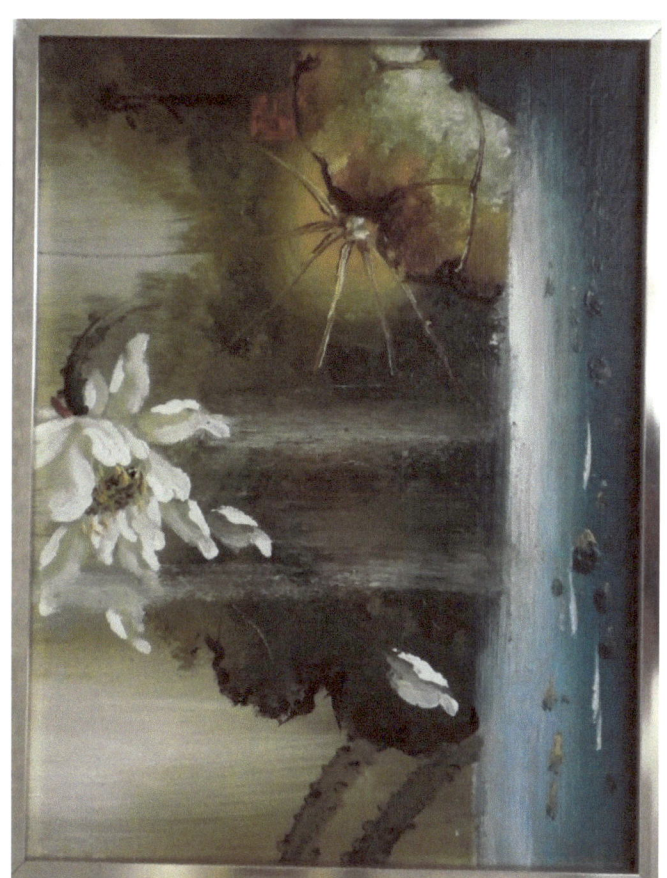

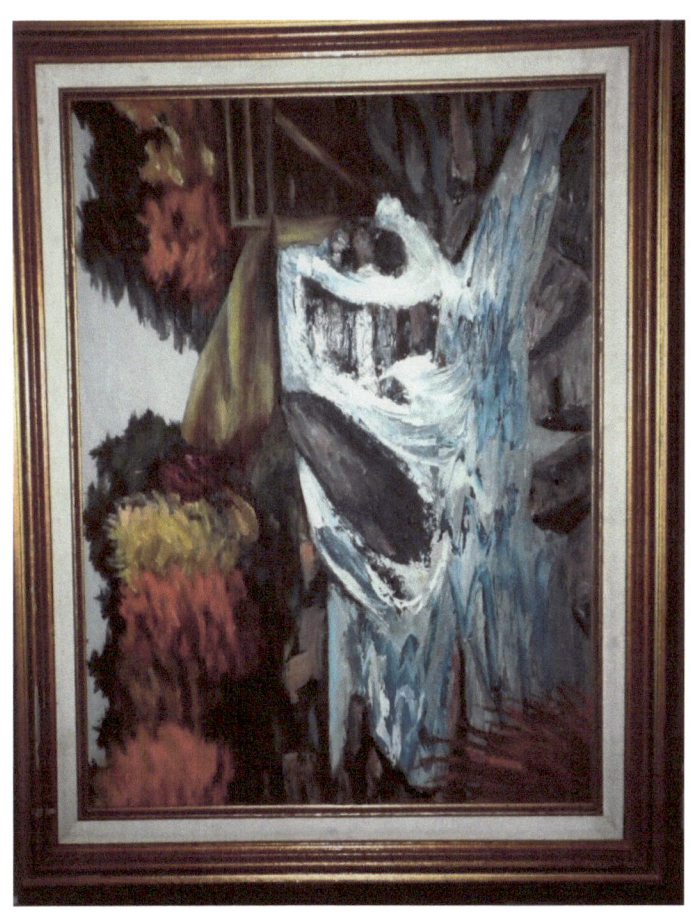

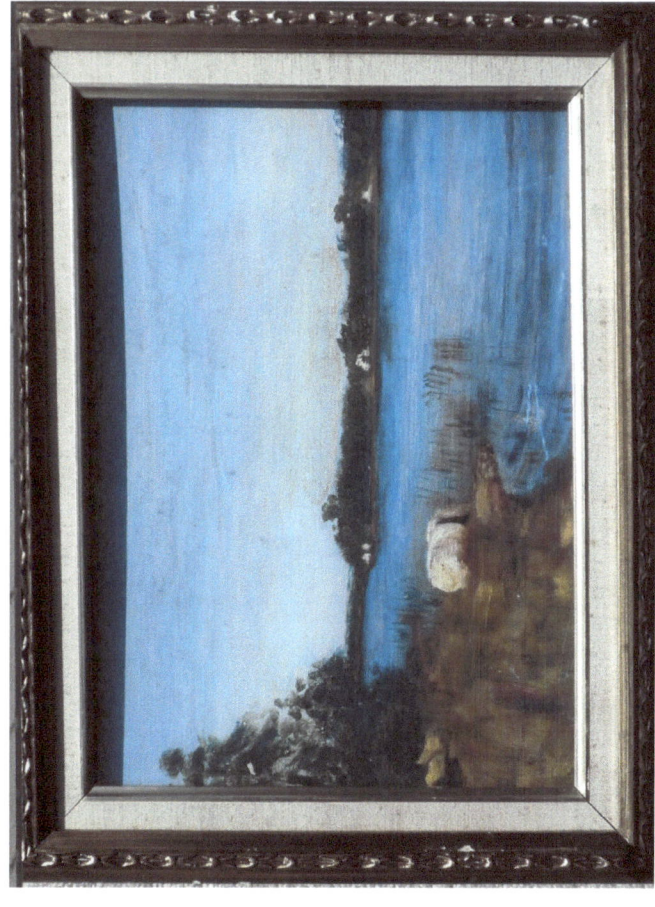

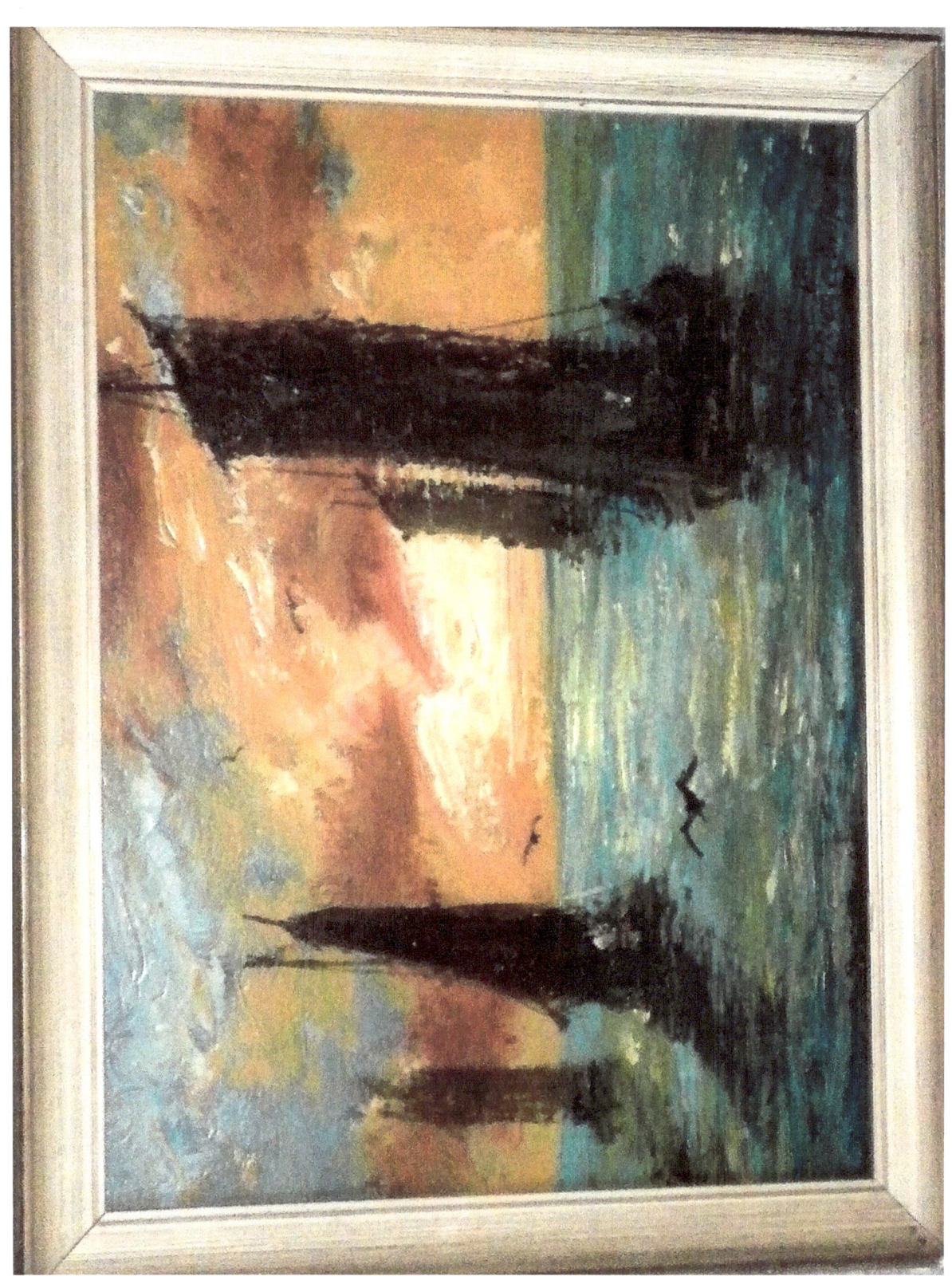

David Devensky – Copyright 2014